The Military System
of the Romans

PLATE 6. PORTES NAVES LONGAE

The Military System of the Romans

Albert Harkness

LEONAUR

The Military System of the Romans
by Albert Harkness

First published under the title
The Military System of the Romans

Leonaur is an imprint of Oakpast Ltd
Copyright in this form © 2011 Oakpast Ltd

ISBN: 978-0-85706-503-2 (hardcover)
ISBN: 978-0-85706-504-9 (softcover)

http://www.leonaur.com

Publisher's Notes

Contents

The Military System of the Romans   7

The Military System of the Romans

1. The Roman Legion, *legio*, was an organized body of Roman soldiers. It contained originally 3,000 infantry and 300 cavalry; but its numerical strength was subsequently increased. In the time of Caesar it consisted entirely of heavy-armed infantry, and probably numbered from 3,500 to 5,000 men.

A legion whose numbers were fully up to the normal standard was called *legio plenissima* and probably contained about 5,000 men. Veteran legions weakened by losses in battle were considerably below this standard.

CAESAR'S ARMY IN GAUL.

2. Caesar's army in Gaul consisted of two distinct parts, the Roman Legions and the auxiliaries.

1. The Roman Legions consisted of heavy-armed soldiers. In general, the *legions* were composed of Roman citizens.

2. The auxiliaries, (some of these were armed, equipped, and disciplined according to the Roman method, while others retained their native arms), consisting of foreign soldiers of various nationalities, served either as cavalry, (Caesar's cavalry was composed chiefly of Gauls; but it contained a few Germans and Spaniards), or as light-armed infantry. Of the auxiliary infantry, the Balearian archers and the Cretan slingers were the most noted. (*The Auxilia of the Roman Imperial Army* by G. L. Cheesman, also published by Leonaur).

3. The entire force at the command of Caesar during his Gallic campaigns seldom, if ever, exceeded 70,000 men. Beginning his work with a single *legion*, the tenth, afterwards so famous in the Gallic wars, he proceeded at once to raise re-enforcements, and soon found himself at the head of an army consisting of six legions and a force of auxiliaries nearly 20,000 strong.

4. The numerical strength of Caesar's army varied somewhat from year to year; but he generally had in his service about 5,000 auxiliary cavalry and from 15,000 to 20,000 auxiliary infantry. The following is a general estimate of the forces at his command during the seven successive campaigns described in the *Commentaries*.

1. In campaign 1, 58 B. C., six *legions*, and about 20,000 auxiliaries,—cavalry and infantry; in all, from 40,000 to 50,000 men.

Caesar found the 10th Legion in Gaul, brought the 7th, 8th, and 9th from their winter-quarters, and enrolled two new *legions*—the 11th and 12th—in Cisalpine Gaul. His auxiliaries consisted of 4,000 cavalry and a large force of light-armed infantry. The number of the latter, not definitely given in the *Commentaries*, has been variously estimated from 15,000 to 30,000. The estimate of Rheinhard is 15,000, that of General von Göler, 30,000.

2. In campaigns 2, 3, and 4, 57, 56, and 55 B. C., eight legions, with the usual force of auxiliaries; in all, from 50,000 to 60,000 men.

For the second campaign Caesar enrolled two new *legions*—the 13th and the 14th. These were added to the six already in his service.

3. In campaign 5, 54 B. C., eight and a half *legions* (subsequently reduced by losses to seven), with the usual force of auxiliaries; in all, from 50,000 to 60,000 men.

Napoleon III. accounts for the half *legion* by assuming that Caesar procured several separate *cohorts* to serve in his fleet in his second expedition into Britain. The five *cohorts* and almost the whole of the 14th Legion were lost under Sabinus and Cotta, among the Eburones.

4. In campaign 6, 53 B. C., ten *legions*, with the usual force of auxiliaries; in all, from 60,000 to 70,000 men.

In preparation for the sixth campaign, Caesar levied two new *legions*—the 14th and the 15th—and obtained another—the 1st—from Pompey. The 14th took the place of the 14th that was lost.

5. In campaign 7, 52 B. C., eleven *legions*, with about 25,000 or 30,000 auxiliaries; in all, not far from 70,000 men.

Caesar entered upon the seventh campaign with ten *legions*; but another—the 6th—was added to the number in the course of the summer. These eleven *legions* were the 1st, 6th, 7th, 8th, 9th, 10th, 11th, 12th, 13th, 14th, and 15th. During this campaign, Caesar probably had a larger force of auxiliaries than at any previous time, as he besought the Aedui to send him all their cavalry and 10,000 infantry, and demanded cavalry and light-armed infantry from subject states in Germany. Moreover, he speaks of 22 *cohorts* of auxiliaries, collected from the province by Lucius Caesar.

HISTORY OF THE ROMAN LEGION.

5. The history of the Roman legion naturally divides itself into three periods.

1. During the first period, the infantry of the *legion* in battle-array stood in the form of a solid *phalanx*, probably from six to eight ranks deep. The division of cavalry, 300 in number, belonging to the *legion*, was generally stationed in front of the *phalanx*.

The unbroken front of this *phalanx* was probably about 1,500 feet long. Its original depth is not known, but Marquardt and Mommsen conjecture that it contained at first six ranks, Rüstow and Köchly that in its later form it contained eight ranks. Livy, I. 43, compares it to the famous Macedonian *phalanx*.

2. During the second period, the infantry of the *legion*

was divided into thirty *maniples*, or companies, which, in battle-array, were arranged in three lines, with intervals between them, as follows:—

Hastati   — — — — — — — — — —

Principes   — — — — — — — — — —

Triarii   — — — — —   — — — —

The change from the *phalanx* to the *legion* of *maniples* is supposed to have been made in the early part of the fourth century before Christ. It is generally ascribed to Camillus, but see Fröhlich, *Kriegführung und Kriegskunst der Römer.* The interval was probably equal to the length of a *maniple.* The *legion* of *maniples* was, doubtless, somewhat slowly developed. The form here given is that described by Polybius. A *legion*, arranged in three lines, of 15 *maniples* each, is mentioned by Livy.

    a. The soldiers in the first line were called *Hastati*; those in the second, *Principes*; and those in the third, *Triarii.* The *Hastati* were comparatively young men, who had seen less service than the soldiers in either of the other lines; the *Principes* were in the full strength of mature manhood; while the *Triarii* were veterans in the service.

    The origin of these terms is doubtful; but it has been suggested that *Principes*, in its original application, probably designated the soldiers who were best armed and equipped; that *Hastati* was a general name for all the heavy-armed soldiers, though finally retained only by those in the first line, *i.e.*, by the inexperienced soldiers; while the others had more specific and honourable titles; and finally, that the *Triarii*, derived from *tres*, were so called from their place in the third line, which was then the post of honour.

    b. Each *maniple* in the *legion* consisted of two divisions, or companies, called *centuries*, each nominally under the command of an officer, called *centurion*; though the *centurion* of the right *century* generally led the whole *maniple*, he was called the first *centurion (centurio prior)*: in his absence, the second *centurion* commanded. In active service, the two *centuries* stood side by side.

The century *(centuria)*, originally a hundred men, probably contained at this time from 60 to 80.

c. The quota of cavalry, 300 in number, due to each *legion* was stationed on the wings. It was divided into ten companies, called *turmae*, which were each sub-divided into three sections, called *decuriae*. Each *decuria* was under the command of a *decurion*.

3. During the third period, including the time of Caesar, the thirty *maniples* of the *legion* were combined into ten groups, of three *maniples* each. This change was made by Marius, about one hundred years before Christ. To this new military body, formed by uniting three *maniples*, the name *cohort* was given. The *legion* thus changed ordinarily stood, when in battle-array, in three lines, with four *cohorts* in the first line, three in the second, and three in the third. For a full account of this order of battle, see **28**. In the time of Caesar the cavalry had ceased to form a part of the *legion*.

PHALANX, MANIPLES, AND COHORTS.

6. The *phalanx*, though it could present a front like a wall to an advancing foe, was yet too unwieldy for the exigencies of the battlefield. To an attempt to remedy this defect the *legion* of maniples owed its origin; but experience soon showed that the division had been carried too far, and that the *maniple* was too small a body to stand alone in the line of battle. Accordingly Marius, in reorganizing the army, proceeded at once to reunite every three *maniples* into a single company, called a *cohort*. The value of the change was soon apparent. The *legion* of *cohorts*, as organized by Marius, and perfected by later generals, while it avoided the special evils of the *phalanx* and of the *legion* of *maniples*, was found, in actual practice, to unite in a large measure the advantages of both.

7. The post of honour in the *phalanx* was awarded to wealth and station; in the other forms of the *legion*, to military achievement and experience. In the *legion* of *maniples*, however, the tried veterans were stationed in the third line as a reserve, to be summoned into action only in cases of special emergency; but in the legion of *cohorts*, they occupied the forefront, and received the first shock of battle. In the *legion* of *cohorts*, the post of honour was the post of danger, while in the *legion* of *maniples* it was a place of comparative security. The Romans had at length learned how much depended upon the first onset.

ARMS OF LEGIONARY SOLDIERS.

8. All *legionary* soldiers were armed with swords and with spears (*hastae*) or javelins (*pila*). The defensive armour, both in the *phalanx* and in the legion of *maniples*, consisted of a coat of mail, a helmet, greaves, and a shield.

In the *legion* of *maniples*, the light-armed soldiers (*velites*), carried a very light spear *(hasta velitaris)*. In the *phalanx*, only the front ranks appeared in full armour. The others being exposed to less danger, dispensed with the coat of mail.

9. In the time of Caesar, the essential articles in a soldier's equipment were as follows:—

1. A plain woollen tunic (*tunica*), with very short sleeves, which scarcely covered half of the upper arm. This was the main article of dress; it extended to the knee, and was girded about the loins.

2. A coat of mail (*lorica*). This was sometimes a simple coat of leather, this seems to have been made, originally, of strips of sole-leather put together in the most substantial manner. Moreover, a metallic breast-plate, 9 or 10 inches square, was sometimes worn under it as represented on the light-armed soldiers in plate 1; and sometimes it was

covered with metal, as seen in the figures of the *legionaries* in the same plate. Observe that flexible bands of steel or bronze encircle the waist; that similar bands extend over the shoulders; and that the upper part of the chest is protected by metallic plates.

3. A thick woollen cloak, or shawl, the *sagum*, sometimes worn by soldiers when not in action. It was thrown over the shoulders in such a manner as to leave the arms comparatively free. It was generally secured by a clasp.

The corresponding garment for the general and the higher officers was the *paludamentum*, which differed from the *sagum* in the fact that it was of larger size, of finer texture, and of more brilliant colour. The *paludamentum* of the commander-in-chief was of purple. For the manner in which the *sagum* and the *paludamentum* were worn, see plates 1 and 2

4. Sandals, or shoes. Of these, there were two or three varieties. The *solea* merely protected the sole of the foot; the *calceus* was an ordinary shoe; the *caliga* was a military shoe, or boot, which covered the whole foot and a part of the ankle. See plates.

5. A helmet, either of bronze (*cassis*), or of leather bound with bronze (*galea*). For the general form and style, see plates 1, 2, and 3. The helmets of the higher officers were generally adorned with plumes of feathers or of horsehair.

Even soldiers of the rank and file are occasionally represented with plumes.

6. Greaves of bronze (*ocreae*). Usually, however, only one was worn, as the left leg was sufficiently protected by the shield.

Soldiers sometimes protected their legs, in cold weather, by wearing strips of cloth, *fasciae*, wound about them. In plate 1, they are represented with tight-fitting breeches, *braccae*, reaching a little below their knees. Whether these were in use in the time of Caesar is very doubtful.

7. A large rectangular shield, the *scutum*, four feet long and two and one-half wide, slightly curved, as seen in plate 1, on the arm of one of the *legionary* soldiers. It was made of wood; but it was covered with leather, and was bound around the edges with iron. It was furnished with a metallic boss (*umbo*), a knob or projection, which not only imparted strength and beauty to the shield, but often caused missiles to glance off from it. For a general view of the arms of the cavalry and of the light-armed infantry, see plate 1.

Shields were ornamented with various devices, as winged thunderbolts, eagles, and laurel wreaths. The name of the soldier and the number of his *cohort* were sometimes inscribed on the inside. Upon the march, the shield was protected from rain and dust by a leathern case drawn over it for the purpose. This was removed before going into battle.

8. The so-called Spanish sword (*gladius Hispanus*), the only sword used by the legions of Caesar. It had a two-edged pointed blade, about two feet long and almost four inches wide, well adapted both for thrusting and for striking, though ordinarily used for thrusting. It was generally worn on the right side, suspended from a belt (*balteus*) passing over the left shoulder, as seen in plate 1; but the higher officers wore it on the left side, suspended from a girdle (*cingulum.*) The sheath and hilt were sometimes richly ornamented.

9. A heavy javelin (*pilum*). This weapon, intended for hurling, not for thrusting, was about six feet and a half long. It consisted of a wooden shaft, upwards of an inch thick and about four feet long, from which projected an iron, from two to three feet long, terminating in a steel head. The *pilum* and the sword were the weapons with which the Roman *legions* conquered the world.

Sword gladius

Sword in sheath

The *pilum* as described by Polybius was 6 feet and 9 inches long, but, from researches recently made, it seems probable that the *pilum* in the time of Caesar was about 6 feet long. The shaft was either round or square. The momentum of the weapon, when hurled by the strong hand of a *legionary* soldier, was very great. It crushed through the shields of the enemy, and, bending under the weight of the blow, could be drawn out only with the greatest difficulty. In no event could it be hurled back upon the *legions*.

It has been estimated that a *pilum* hurled with ordinary force would cut through an oak board half an inch thick, lined with sheet iron, and that it would undoubtedly penetrate both the shield and the coat of mail. For a full account of this weapon, see Marquardt, *Römische Staatsverwaltung*, vol. ii.; Jähns, *Geschichte des Kriegswesens*, Guhl und Koner, *Das Leben der Griechen und Homer*; and Lindenschmit, *Tract und Bewaffnung des Römischen Heeres*.

The corresponding weapons of the Gauls were the *gaesum* and the sword. The former was a heavy javelin or spear, used mostly as a missile. The Gallic swords were very long, but without points; well adapted for striking but not for thrusting. Livy, XXII. 46, characterizes them as *gladii perlongi ac sine mucronibus*.

The Gallic helmet, with its large bushy plume, was intended to give the wearer the appearance of superhuman size. Sometimes, according to Diodorus, horns or frightful figures of beasts or birds projected above it. The Gauls wore breastplates or coats of mail, and carried shields, which are described as very large (*vasta scuta*) though not very wide (*ad amplitudinem corporum parum lata*).

For the arms and the general appearance of Gallic soldiers, infantry and cavalry, see plate 4.

Military Service. Pay of Soldiers.

10. Originally the Roman army was simply the state temporarily in arms. Each citizen armed and supported himself as he was merely doing his own work. Campaigns in those days were of short duration; and the citizen, after having discharged the duties of the soldier for a few weeks, returned to his home. Afterwards, military service was regarded as a tax which every citizen might occasionally be called upon to pay to the state, for the protection of life and property. But about 400 B. C., when Rome began to be involved in more protracted wars, a small allowance was made from the public treasury to furnish the army with supplies.

In the time of Caesar, however, service in the army, which had previously been an occasional duty required of all citizens, had become a permanent profession. Young men of vigour and enterprise entered the army either to become professional soldiers or to qualify themselves for the high offices of state, for which only those were eligible who had served a definite number of campaigns. The soldiers received regular pay, fully equal to that of labourers in Rome; while their perquisites, in the form of booty and presents, were by no means unimportant.

The *legionary* soldier probably received, *per annum*, about 240 *denarii*, a little less than 50 dollars. The pay of the *centurion* was twice as much as that of the common soldier.

11. The soldiers received their pay once in four months, from which a small deduction was made, for supplies furnished them by the state.

The deduction in the time of Polybius was only one-thirtieth part of the pay, and though, in consequence of the higher price of grain, it was somewhat larger in the time of Caesar, it was still very inconsiderable. Thus the pay of a Roman soldier was much higher, relatively to the cost of living, than that of a soldier in a modern European army. The auxiliaries received army-rations, but their pay came from their own people.

The regular allowance of wheat, per month, for each man in the rank and file was a bushel, 4 *modii*; for a *centurion*, two bushels. Supplies were furnished twice a month, half the monthly allowance at a time. For a discussion of the general subject of supplies for the army, and the pay of soldiers, see Sonklar, *Abhan-*

dlung über die Heeresverwaltung der alten Römer.

12. The recruit was required to bring to the service a sound and vigorous body; but no definite stature seems to have been prescribed. He entered at once upon a long and severe course of professional training. The success of the Roman arms was due largely to discipline and military drill.

THE LEGION IN THE TIME OF CAESAR.

13. In the time of Caesar, the regular or normal strength of a Roman legion when mustered into service was probably about 5,000 men. This is the estimate of Lange and of General von Göler. Mommsen estimates a full legion in the time of Marius at 6,000. Napoleon III. gives the same estimate for the legions engaged in the battle near Bibracte. The actual numerical strength of Caesar's *legions* in Gaul, after years of hard service, was, of course, far below this standard. Indeed, it is doubtful whether the muster-roll of some of the veteran *legions* in the later Gallic campaigns would much exceed 2,000. Rüstow estimates the average numerical strength of the legions in Gaul at 3,600. Kraner's estimate is a little lower, from 3,000 to 3,600, and Mommsen's considerably higher, from 3,500 to 5,000.

14. The legion consisted of ten *cohorts.* To understand, therefore, the organization and action of the legion as a whole, we must first get a clear idea of the size, form, and movements of the cohort, which is the tactical unit on which everything depends.

15. It seems safe to assume that the standard numerical strength of the *cohort* was about 500; but that the actual strength of Caesar's *cohorts* in Gaul did not upon the average much exceed 360.

16. It will be remembered that the *cohort* was formed by uniting three *maniples*, and that each *maniple* consisted of two centuries, each under the command of a *centurion.* When the cohort was in battle-array, the men probably stood in rank and file as follows:—

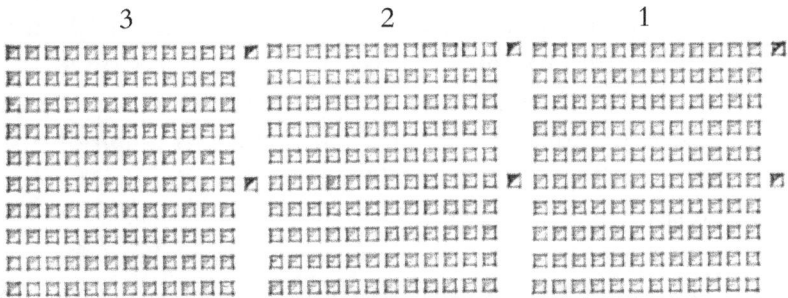

COHORT IN LINE OF BATTLE. FRONT 120 FEET, DEPTH 40 FEET.

17. Here 1, 2, and 3 represent the three *maniples* united to form the *cohort*. Number 1, on the right wing, is the veteran *maniple* of the *cohort*, and holds the post of honour; *maniple* 2, in the centre, consists of soldiers who, though in mature manhood, have not yet attained the rank of veterans; while *maniple* 3 contains those who have seen the least service of all. Originally, *maniple* 1 was designated by the name *Triarii*, or *Pilani*; 2, by the name *Principes*; and 3, by the name *Hastati*; but as these names do not occur in the Commentaries on the Gallic War, and as they have all lost their original signification, the simple numerals, first, second, and third, seem to be the most appropriate designations of the *maniples*, especially as they indicate their true rank and order.

Thus it appears probable that Marias, in organizing the cohort, took one *maniple* from each of the three lines in which the *legion* had previously been marshalled for battle, naturally awarding the post of honour, on the right wing, to the veteran maniple, the *Triarii*, also called *Pilani*; the centre to the *Principes*, and the left wing to the *Hastati*. See **6.**

These ancient names could not fail to be misleading to the learner, if applied to the *maniples* in the *cohort*; as *Hastati*, for instance, means armed with the *hasta*, while the third *maniple*, to which it was applied, was armed not with the *hasta*, but with the *pilum*; again, *Principes* means holding the first place or rank, and yet the second *maniple* did not hold either the first place or the first rank.

19

18. Each *maniple* contained 120 men, arranged in ten ranks of twelve men each, in other words, each rank contained 12 men, and each file 10. The space allowed to a soldier was three feet wide and four feet deep, *i.e.* each file occupied 3 feet, and each rank 4 feet. The first five ranks formed the first *century*,—the *century*, originally called *centuria*, is called *ordo* in the *Commentaries*—the last five the second *century*.

The two *centurions* occupied positions at the right of the *centuries* which they commanded. For their use the space of four feet was left at the right of each *maniple*, as indicated in the figure under **16**. The *centurion* at the extreme right in front was the chief *centurion* of the *cohort*. He not only led his own *century*, but was also charged with the general command of the entire *cohort*.

19. The length or front of the *maniple*, occupied as it was by twelve men and one *centurion*, was 40 feet, *i.e.* 12 x 3 + 4 = 40, while the depth, or file, occupied by ten men, was also 40 feet, *i.e.* 10 x 4 = 40.

Thus the *maniple* was 40 feet square, and three such squares placed side by side formed the *cohort*, which was accordingly 120 feet long and 40 deep. The arrangement here given, in which the three *maniples* stand side by side in the *cohort*, while the second *century* stands directly behind the first in each *maniple*, has been quite generally accepted, but General von Göler places the two *centuries*, two ranks deep, side by side in the *maniple*, and stations the first *maniple* at the head of the *cohort*, the second directly behind the first, and the third directly behind the second.

20. The following figure represents a *cohort* in various positions as in line of battle and on the march. A rectangle with a diagonal across it may represent any company or body of soldiers, as a *century*, *maniple*, or *cohort*. In this figure it represents a *century*. The diagonal is drawn from the right of the front to the left the rear.

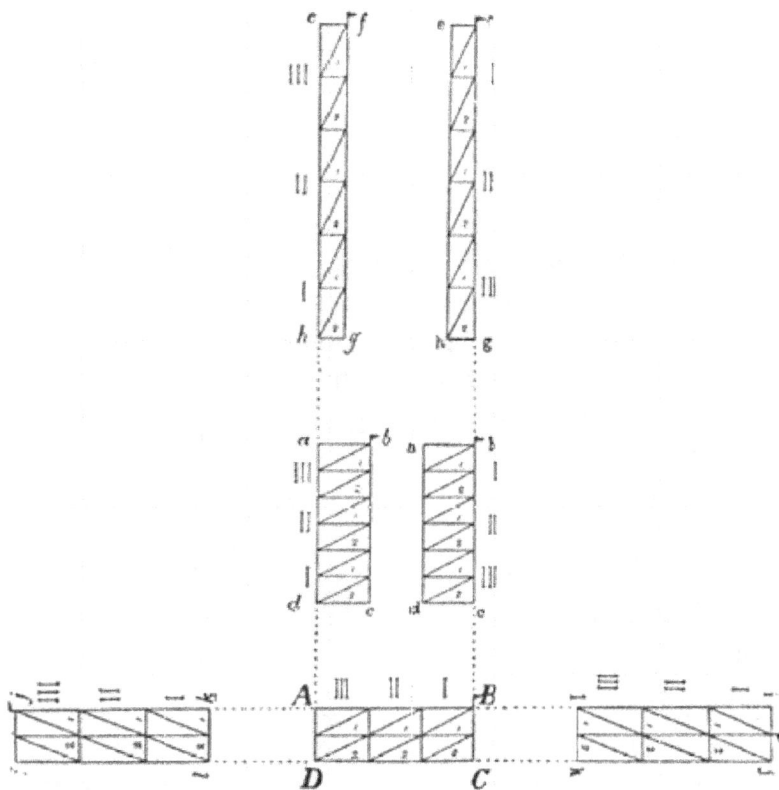

1. ABCD represents a *cohort* 360 strong in line of battle.

2. abcd, the same *cohort* marching in column of *centuries*, with the first *maniple* in front.

3. *abcd*, the same column with the third *maniple* in front.

4. efgh, the *cohort* in column of *centuries* of half the usual width and twice the usual length, with the first *maniple* in front.

5. *efgh,* the same column with the third *maniple* in front.

6. ijkl, *cohort* in column of *maniples*, with the first *maniple* in front.

7. *ijkl*, the same column with the third *maniple* in front.

21. In 'abcd ' and 'abcd' the column is called a column of *centuries*, because it consists of the six *centuries* of the *cohort*, placed one directly behind another. The column thus formed was 40 feet wide and 120 feet long. The column of *centuries* was the usual order of march, and was formed from the line of battle in two ways, as follows:—

1. The right wing, or *maniple* 1, marched straight forward; *maniple* 2 fell directly in the rear of 1, and *maniple* 3 in the rear of 2. This movement gives 'abcd,' already mentioned, as a *cohort* marching in column of *centuries*, with the right wing, or *maniple* 1, in front, *i.e.*, the *maniple* which in battle-array formed the right wing of the *cohort*, became the head of the column.

2. The left wing, or *maniple* 3, marched straight forward, *maniple* 2 fell directly in the rear of 3, and *maniple* 1 in the rear of 2. This movement gives 'abcd' a *cohort* marching in column of *centuries* with the left wing, or *maniple* 3, in front.

22. It will be observed that the column of *centuries* is 40 feet wide, having exactly the width of a *maniple*. This seems to have been the favourite column on the march through an open country, or upon highways of sufficient width. Caesar's famous bridge over the Rhine was 40 feet wide, and thus exactly adapted to the width of an army marching in column of *centuries*. Many roads in Gaul, however, were not more than 15 or 20 feet wide. In what form could a Roman army march over such roads? In the regular column of *centuries*, the 60 men belonging to a *century* were arranged in 5 ranks of 12 men each; but the *century* was sometimes arranged in 10 ranks of 6 men each. Such an arrangement is represented in 'efgh.'

Here each *century*, each *maniple*, and the entire *cohort* have only half the usual width, but twice the usual length. The column has only 6 men abreast, and is only 18 feet wide, or, including the *centurion*, 22 feet. By adopting a close order, the width could be reduced in case of need to 18, or even 15 feet. The regular or normal width of Roman roads was 18 feet. See Jähns, *Geschichte des Kriegswesens.*

23. In 'ijkl' and '*ijkl*' the column is called a column of *maniples*, because it consists of the three *maniples* of the *cohort* placed one directly behind another. Here the two *centuries* of each maniple stand abreast. In 'ijkl' the *cohort* is said to be marching by the right flank, because in forming this column from the line of battle, each man turns, or faces to the right, and thus the file which formed the right flank in battle-array becomes the front rank of the column. In '*ijkl*' the *cohort* is said to be marching by the left flank, because in forming this column, each man turns or faces to the left. 2

When the *cohort* marches by the right flank, the right wing, or *maniple* 1, becomes the head of the column; when it marches by the left flank, the left wing, or *maniple* 3, becomes the head.

24. It will be observed that the column of *maniples* will be considerably longer than the column of *centuries*, as it contains more ranks. In this column, each *maniple*, as it has 12 ranks, will be 48 feet long, or, if we allow 4 feet for the *centurion*, who probably kept his place at the head of his *century*, it will be 52 feet long. This gives 156 feet as the length of the *cohort* marching in a column of *maniples*. As this column was formed from the line of battle by simply facing to the right or left, the depth of the cohort, 40 feet, naturally became the width of the column, but in marching, as there were only 10 men abreast, the width was often reduced to 30 feet.

Upon narrow roads the column of *maniples*, like the column of *centuries*, was sometimes reduced to one-half its usual width by doubling its length. Such a column had only 5 men abreast, and could without difficulty march over a road 15, or even 12, feet wide. In forming this column from the regular column of *maniples*, one of the two *centuries* in each *maniple* marched straight on while the other fell in its rear.

The learner should carefully distinguish between a column of *centuries*, as seen in 'abcd' and '*abcd*, and a column of *maniples*, as seen in 'ijkl' and '*ijkl.*' In the former, the column is an unbroken series of *centuries*, arranged one behind another; while in the latter, the two *centuries* of each *maniple* stand abreast.

25. The following summary gives the length and width of the *cohort* in different positions:—

	Front.	Depth.
1. *Cohort* in line of battle	120 feet.	40 feet
2. *Cohort* in column of *centuries*	40 "	120 "
3. *Cohort* in column of *centuries*, with 6 files[1]	18 to 22 "	240 "
4. *Cohort* in column of *maniples*[2]	30 to 40 "	144 to 156 "
5. Cohort in column of *maniples*, with 5 files	15 to 20 "	288 to 300 "

26. As an army on the march was liable to attack, it was often necessary to form the line of battle from the line of march. If the enemy appeared on the flank, this was most easily effected from the column of *maniples* marching in loose order, *i.e.*, with 40 feet front. The simple command, "Halt, front," was all that was needful. Thus if an enemy appeared on the right flank of a column of *maniples*, as represented by 'ijkl,' it was only necessary for each man to face to the right to place the *cohort* in line of battle; but if the enemy appeared on the left flank, it was of course necessary for the men to face to the left.

If, however, the enemy appeared in front, the line of battle was most readily formed from the column of *centuries*. Thus if the enemy appeared in front of the column of *centuries* represented by 'abcd,' *maniple* 1 halted, *maniple* 2 placed itself at the left of 1, and *maniple* 3 at the left of 2.

LEGION IN LINE OF BATTLE.

27. As a *legion* is only an aggregate of ten *cohorts* properly arranged, we may now apply to the *legion* what we have already learned in regard to the *cohort*. A legion in line of battle consists

---

1. The full allowance would be 22 feet, 18 for the 6 files, and 4 for the centurion, reduced in case of need to 18 or less.

2. In loose order, 40 feet; but this gives each man 4 feet; if we reduce the allowance to 3 feet, the front of the column becomes 30 feet.

simply of ten *cohorts*, each in its proper position and in battle-array; a *legion* on the march, of ten *cohorts* marching in due order, and with the proper intervals between them.

28. But we have already learned, (see **5,** 3), that in a *legion* in battle-array, the ten *cohorts* were arranged in three lines, with four *cohorts* in the first or front line, three in the second, and three in the third, as follows:—

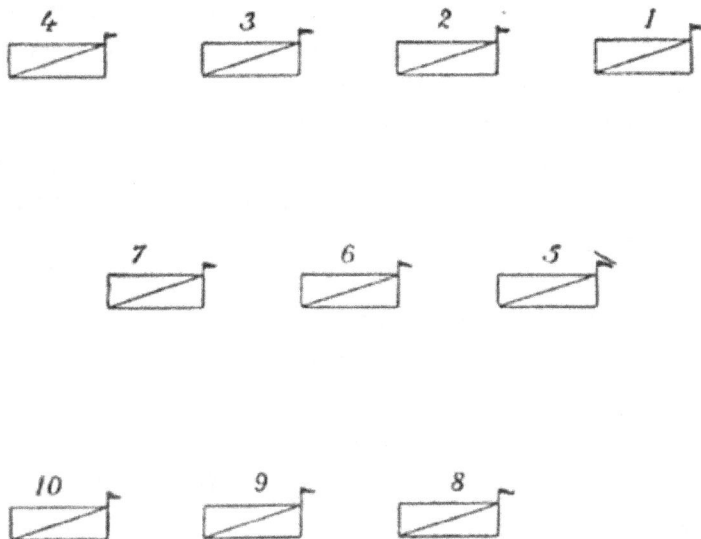

LEGION IN LINE OF BATTLE

This order of battle is generally supposed to be the *acies triplex*, so often mentioned by Caesar, but General von Göler claims that the *acies triplex* refers, not to the three lines of *cohorts*, but to the three great divisions of an army, *viz.*, the main body or the central division, and the two wings.

29. Observe that the *cohorts* are arranged with intervals between them, that the *cohorts* in the second line are directly behind the intervals in the first, and that the *cohorts* in the third line are directly behind the intervals in the second. As the third line was held as a reserve, and was not often called into action, the exact position of the *cohorts* seems not to have been as definitely determined as in the other lines. The order here given has been adopted from Rüstow. Göler arranges the *cohorts* as follows:—

4		3		2		1
	7		6		5	
10			9			8

The *cohorts* are numbered from 1 to 10, according to the rank and military experience of the *centurions* and soldiers. Thus promotions both of *centurions* and of men were from the tenth *cohort* to the ninth, from the ninth to the eighth, from the eighth to the seventh, and so on through all the *cohorts* to the first. A position in the front line is more honourable than in either of the others, while in either line a position on the right wing is more honourable than on the left. The first *cohort*, holding the post of honour, is on the extreme right of the front line, while the tenth, holding the lowest rank in the *legion*, is on the extreme left of the third line.

30. The interval between the *cohorts* in each line was 120 feet, the length of a *cohort*, but the interval between the lines was probably 240 or 250 feet. Thus the front or length of a *legion* in battle-array was 840 feet, while its depth from the front of the first line of *cohorts* to the rear of the third line was from 600 to 620 feet. The front, or length, of the *legion* was made up of the length of four *cohorts* and of three intervals, each 120 feet. It was therefore 7 x 120 = 840 feet. The depth was made up of the depth of the three lines of *cohorts*, each 40 feet, and two intervals, each 240 or 250 feet, *i.e.*, it was 120 + 480 or 500 = 600 or 620 feet.

31. When an army consisting of several *legions* was marshalled in order of battle, each *legion* was arranged in three lines, as already described, and the several *legions* were separated by intervals, probably varying in length with the nature of the ground, but seldom less than 120 feet, the length of a *cohort*. If we assume that this interval was 120 feet, we shall find that the front of Caesar's line of battle on the Axona, with six *legions*, was 5,640 feet and its depth, 600 feet, *i.e.* 6 x 840 + 5 x 120 = 5,040 + 600 = 5,640 feet. Thus the line of battle of an army of six *legions*, numbering in all about 25,000 men, was considerably more than a mile long and almost an eighth of a mile deep, and occupied upwards of 75 acres of ground.

OFFICERS IN A ROMAN ARMY.

32. In a Roman army engaged in an important work like the conquest of Gaul, the regular officers were the commander-in-chief, the lieutenant-generals, the *quaestor*, the military tribunes, the centurions, the *praefects*, and the *decurions*.

33. The commander-in-chief, called *dux belli* or *imperator*, had in his own province almost unlimited military power. He was clothed with the full measure of authority which belongs to a commander-in-chief in modern warfare.

34. The lieutenant-generals, *legati*, were the highest officers in the army under the commander-in-chief. They were all of senatorial rank and received their appointment from the senate. In the absence of the commander-in-chief, they assumed his duties. They were sometimes placed in command of important detachments detailed for special service. In the battle with Ariovistus, Caesar placed one of his *legions* under the command of his *quaestor* and each of the other five under the command of one of his lieutenants.

35. The *quaestor* had charge of the military chest, and was the quartermaster of the army. He had the rank of a lieutenant-general, *legatus*, and was sometimes entrusted with a command in battle.

36. The special officers of the separate *legions* were the military *tribunes* and the *centurions*.

37. Each *legion* had six military *tribunes, tribuni militum*, who formerly commanded in rotation, two at a time for a period of two months. The two *tribunes* commanded by turns, each for one day. See Marquardt, *Römische Staatsverwaltung*, Vol. II., p. 352; also Jähns, *Geschichte des Kriegswesens*.

In the army in Gaul, however, the *tribunes* were mostly young men of wealth and social position whom Caesar, from personal friendship or political considerations, had selected from the equestrian order and placed upon his staff. They had little military experience or knowledge, and were accordingly incompetent to take the general command of a legion in battle, though they were sometimes entrusted with the command of small detachments detailed for special service. In general, they administered the internal affairs of the *legion*. They served as staff-officers to the commander-in-chief and as adjutants to the lieutenant-generals and the *quaestor*.

38. Each *legion* had also 60 *centurions*. According to Göler, there were 120 *centurions* in each *legion*, but he includes in this number the 60 assistant *centurions*, called *optiones*. These officers were in general men of large military experience, who had been promoted from the ranks, as a reward of good service. They were the real commanders, not only of *centuries*, but also of *maniples* and *cohorts*, and, in a certain sense, under the *legatus*, of the *legion* as a whole. The two *centurions* in each *maniple* differed from each other in rank; the first, called *centurio prior*, commanded the *maniple*, while the second, called *centurio posterior*, served as his adjutant. The first *centurion* of the first *maniple* commanded the *cohort*, and the first *centurion* of the first *maniple* of the first *cohort*, called *primi pili centurio*, or *primipilus*, was the chief *centurion* of the *legion*, and had much to do with the general command.

39. The Romans in their military system seem to have aimed to stimulate ambition and reward fidelity. An enterprising recruit who on entering the service took his place at the very foot of the *legion*, in the second *century* of the third *maniple* of the tenth *cohort*, had before him a long career of advancement in the rank and file of the army, and if, by bravery and fidelity, he succeeded in attaining the coveted office of *centurion*, the prospect of promotion was still before him. He might hope to rise from *maniple* to *maniple*, and from *cohort* to *cohort*, until, in the end, having passed through all the grades of honour, he should become the chief *centurion*, the *primipilus* of the *legion*. This was the height of his ambition, the goal of his aspirations.

40. The exact order of promotion is still a disputed question. According to Rüstow, the six *centurions* of each *cohort* formed a separate class, the *centurions* of the first *cohort* forming the first class, those of the tenth *cohort* the tenth class. Thus there were ten classes, and each class contained six *centurions*. To determine the rank of a *centurion*, we must know to which *cohort* he belonged, to which *maniple* in the *cohort*, and to which *century* in the *maniple*. Thus the full designation of his rank required the use of three separate titles:

(1), an ordinal numeral, as *primus*, if he belonged to the first *cohort*, *secundus*, if he belonged to the second;

(2), the word *pilus*, if he belonged to the first *maniple* in his *cohort*, *princeps*, if he belonged to the second, and *hastatus*, if he belonged to the third; and:

(3) *prior*, if he belonged to the first *century* in his *maniple*, and *posterior*, if he belonged to the second. Thus *primus pilus prior*, applied to a *centurion*, denotes that he commanded the first *century* of the first *maniple* of the first *cohort*, in other words, that he was the chief *centurion* of the *legion*; *decimus hastatus posterior* denotes that he commanded the second *century* of the third *maniple* of the tenth *cohort*, i.e., that he was the lowest *centurion* in the *legion*, while *quintus princeps prior* denotes that he commanded the first *century* of the second *maniple* of the fifth *cohort*.

This is probably the prevailing view among scholars. According to Göler, however, the first *centurion* of each *cohort* belonged to the first class, the second to the second class, the third to the third class, and so on until all the *centurions* were classified. Thus each class consisted of ten *centurions*, one from each *cohort*, and there were as many classes as there were *centurions* in a *cohort, i. e.*, there were six classes of the regular *centurions*, While, therefore, Rüstow divides the 60 regular *centurions* of a *legion* into ten classes, of six *centurions* each, Göler divides them into six classes, of ten each. In the same manner, Göler divides the 60 assistants or sub-*centurions*, *optiones*, into six classes, of ten each, making in all twelve classes.

41. The *centurions* of the first class, called sometimes *primorum ordinum centuriones*, and sometimes simply *primi ordines*, enjoyed certain honours and privileges not often accorded to the other *centurions*. As a general rule, they alone of the *centurions* were invited by the commander to seats in all councils of war in company with the lieutenants and the military *tribunes*.

42. The *praefects, praefecti*, commanded divisions of auxiliaries, either infantry or cavalry. The *praefects* in the army of Caesar in Gaul were mostly young men who had seen little military service.

43. The *decurions* commanded small companies of cavalry. Each company, or troop, called *turma*, numbering thirty horse, was divided into three sections, called *decuriae*, each under the command of a *decurion*; but the first, or senior, *decurion* commanded not only his own *decuria*, but also the entire *turma*.

Order of March.

44. The usual order of march was either the simple column, *agmen pilatum*, or the line of battle, *acies instructa*. The square, *agmen quadratum*, was resorted to only in extreme cases.

Legions Marching in Column—*Agmen Pilatum.*

45. A *cohort* in column of centuries, as we have already seen (**25**), has a front of 40 feet, with a depth of 120 feet. If the column was formed from the right, the first *cohort* led, and was followed by the others in the order of their numbers, but if the column was formed from the left, the tenth *cohort* led and was followed by the others in the inverse order of their numbers, *i.e.*, the ninth, eighth, etc.

46. On the march, the *cohorts* are supposed to have been separated from each other by an interval of 20 or 30 feet. Assuming an interval of 20 feet, we find that a *legion*, marching in column of *centuries*, with a front of 40 feet, was 1,400 feet long, and with a front of 20 feet, 2,600 feet long. The length of a column of full width was 10 x 120 feet + 10 x 20 feet = 1,400 feet, and the length of a column of half the usual width was 10 x 240 feet + 10 x 20 feet = 2600 feet. This estimate includes the interval of 20 feet between the last *cohort* of the *legion* and the first *cohort* of the next.

47. In general, every Roman soldier carried his own personal baggage. The different articles, consisting of clothing, cooking utensils, and rations for one, two, or more weeks, weighing, probably, in the aggregate, from 30 to 50 pounds, were carefully put up in packages, *sarcinae*, and firmly secured to a rod, as represented in plate 1. On the march, the rod was carried on the shoulder. This arrangement for the convenience of the soldier, introduced by Marius, was called from him *mulus Marianus*, the "mule of Marius." It was simply a primitive knapsack.

48. The general baggage of the army, called *impedimenta*, comprising tents, tools, and supplies of various kinds, was carried by beasts of burden, *jumenta*. According to Rüstow's estimate, the length of the baggage-train of a *legion* marching in a column of *centuries* of full width, was 650 feet, and that of a *legion* marching in a column of *centuries* of half the usual width, 1,300 feet. This estimate allows to each *legion* 520 beasts of burden, arranged in 65 full ranks, with 8 animals in a rank, and gives 10 feet to each rank.

49. We have just seen (**46**) that a *legion* without baggage-train, in a column of *centuries* of full width, was 1,400 feet long, and in a column of half the usual width, 2,600 feet long. Including the baggage-train, therefore, the entire length of the column of full width must have been about 2,050 feet, or two-fifths of a mile, and the entire length of the column of half the usual width, about 3,900 feet, or almost four-fifths of a mile. The column of maniples of any given force would be about one-fifth longer than the column of *centuries*.

50. Before the battle of the Sabis, Caesar had eight *legions* on the march. The length of a column of *centuries*, containing such a force, would be 16,400 feet, upwards of three miles, if the column was of full width; and 31,200 feet, upwards of six miles, if the column was of half the usual width.

MARCHING IN LINE OF BATTLE—*ACIES INSTRUCTA*.

51. A *legion* marching in line of battle was usually arranged in three parallel lines of cohorts; but these lines might be formed in two different ways, as follows:

1. The three lines of *cohorts* which constituted the usual order of battle, the *triplex acies*, formed the three parallel columns. Thus *cohorts* 1, 2, 3, and 4 formed the first column, 5, 6, and 7 the second, and 8, 9, and 10 the third, as seen in figure 2, on the following page.

In forming these columns, each man faced to the right or left, and marched by the right or left flank. Each *cohort* marched in column of *maniples*. In an army of several *legions*, marching in this order, the second *legion* was placed directly in the rear of the first, the third directly in the rear of the second, and so on to the end of the column. Thus the whole army marched in three parallel columns of *maniples*. If the enemy appeared on either flank, the columns halted, each man faced to the right or left, as the case required, the *cohorts* separated, and the whole army was in battle-array. This order of march was usually adopted when the enemy was expected on the flank.

2. When the enemy was expected in front, the *legion* marched straight forward with its *cohorts* in column of *centuries*: the three *cohorts* on the right wing of the *legion*, *viz.*, 1, 5, and 8, fell into line and formed the right column,

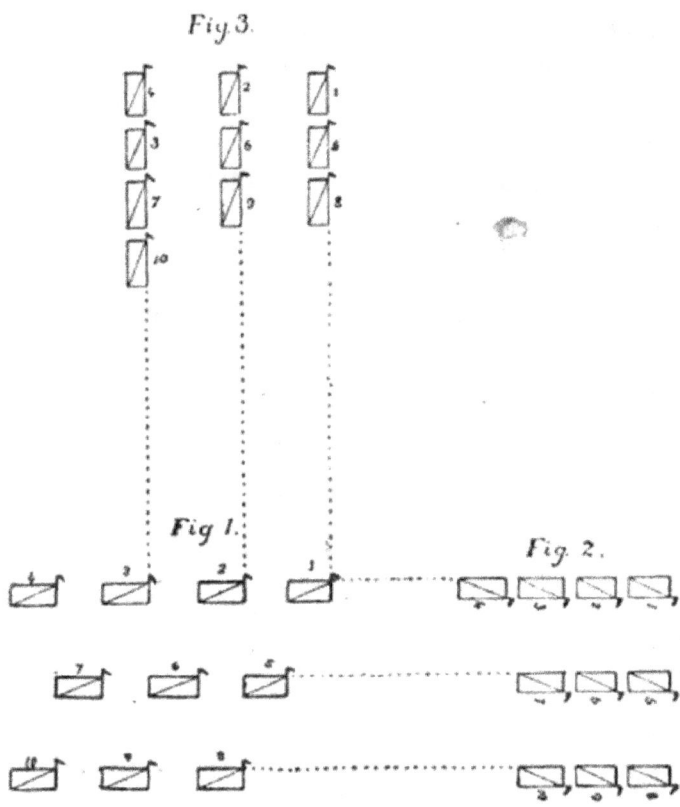

Fig. 3.

Fig. 1.

Fig. 2.

FIGURE 1 REPRESENTS A LEGION IN ORDER OF BATTLE.

FIGURE 2, A LEGION MARCHING IN ORDER OF BATTLE, WITH ITS COHORTS IN COLUMN OF MANIPLES.

FIGURE 3, A LEGION MARCHING IN ORDER OF BATTLE, WITH ITS COHORTS IN COLUMN OF CENTURIES.

the central *cohorts*, 2, 6, and 9, formed the middle column, and the left *cohorts*, 3, 4, 7, and 10, the left column, as seen in figure 3, above. In an army of several *legions*, marching in this order, the *legions* were all placed abreast, and there were three times as many columns as there were *legions*. Thus an army of 6 *legions* marched in 18 parallel columns. To form the line of battle from these columns, it was only necessary for each *cohort* to arrange its own *maniples* in order of battle, as already described (**26**), and then take its proper station in the line.

52. The square, the *agmen quadratum*, was adopted on the march only in the presence of an overwhelming force of the enemy. In regard to its exact formation, there is some diversity of opinion. According to Rüstow, the ten *cohorts* of each *legion* formed a rectangle enclosing the baggage, as seen in the accompanying figure.

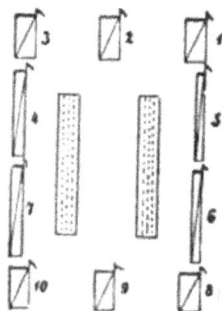

Agmen Quadratum.

Cohorts 1, 2, and 3, in column of *centuries*, formed the vanguard; *cohorts* 8, 9, and 10, also in column of *centuries*, formed the rearguard; while 5 and 6, in columns of *maniples* of 5 files, formed the right wing, and 4 and 7, also in column of *maniples* with 5 files, formed the left wing.

53. In an army on the march, we recognize three parts, more or less distinct:—

1. The vanguard, the head of the column, *primum agmen*.

2. The main body of the army, *exercitus, omnes copiae*.

3. The rearguard, the rear, *novissimum agmen*.

54. The special organization of the different parts of the column, and indeed the entire order of march, depended largely upon the direction of the movement in relation to the enemy.

Order of March in Advancing.

55. In advance movements in the Gallic campaigns, the vanguard of Caesar's army ordinarily consisted of cavalry and light-armed infantry, together with the *tribunes, centurions*, and *legionaries* entrusted with the duty of selecting and measuring off the ground for the camp. It was its special duty to reconnoitre the country, to take note of all hostile preparations, to gain tidings of the enemy, and in due time to select a suitable place for the camp. From the van, detachments of cavalry were sent out in various directions, sometimes to great distances. It was by means of such reconnoitring parties that Caesar obtained tidings of the movements of Ariovistus, while he was yet twenty-four miles distant.

56. The main body of the army followed the van at a convenient distance. It marched in column of centuries, each legion with its baggage directly behind it; but the last legion probably detailed a few cohorts to protect its baggage, and in that event the cohorts thus detailed formed the rearguard of the army. In this order of march, the legions, thus separated by their baggage, were exposed in case of an attack to great peril; they were accordingly said to be *impeditae*, entangled or impeded by baggage, *impedimentum*.

57. In advancing in the presence of the enemy the *legions* marched either in column of *centuries*, with collected baggage, or in order of battle. With the first arrangement, the main body, consisting of three-fourths of all the *legions*, followed close upon the advance-guard, and was itself immediately followed by the collected baggage-train of the army. The few remaining *legions* formed the rearguard of the column.

In this order of march, the *legions* were comparatively ready for action, and were said to be *expeditae*, disentangled, or free from encumbrance; but the individual soldiers were still *impediti*, and in case of an attack, they required time to dispose of their personal baggage, to remove the coverings from their shields, to put on their helmets, to adjust their field-badges, and, in a word, to prepare for action. In such an emergency, it was the special duty of the advance-guard to secure for them the needful time by engaging the enemy, and thus retarding his movements.

58. Sometimes in advancing in the immediate presence of the enemy, if the ground permitted, the several *legions* marched abreast, each in three parallel columns in order of battle. For the special formation and arrangement of the columns, see **51.** In this order of march, every soldier, free from his baggage, and fully armed and equipped, was *expeditus*, ready for immediate action.

ORDER OF MARCH IN RETREAT.

59. The order of march in retreat was usually the simple column of *centuries* with collected baggage. The vanguard, consisting of a *legion* or more, started in advance, with the entire baggage-train of the army; at a suitable distance behind marched the other *legions*, followed by the rearguard, consisting of cavalry, archers, and slingers.

60. In cases of extreme peril, the *agmen quadratum*, already explained (**52**), was adopted in retreat. In such an emergency, all the *legions* of the army were sometimes massed around their baggage in a single square or rectangle, and sometimes each *legion* enclosed its own baggage, as explained in **52.** The cavalry, archers, and slingers, remaining outside of the squares, served as skirmishers.

ORDER OF MARCH IN FLANK MOVEMENTS.

61. Flank marches were always made in order of battle. An army is said to make a flank movement when it passes near the flank of the enemy or marches in a direction parallel to his line of march The *legions* generally marched in three columns of *maniples*. For the formation of these columns, see **51**, 1. In an open country, the cavalry, archers, and slingers, marched on the flank toward the enemy, while the baggage-train was stationed on the other flank. In special cases, each *legion* was followed by its own baggage.

62. The day's march of a Roman army in the field began at four or five o'clock in the morning and continued till about midday. Most of the afternoon was occupied in fortifying the camp and in attending to various duties connected with camp-life. The distance usually accomplished in a day does not seem to have differed much from an ordinary day's march of modern armies. The average distance was probably about fifteen or sixteen miles. Forced marches (*magna itinera*) were, of course, much longer. In one instance, Caesar marched about fifty miles in a little more than twenty-four hours; but this was an exceptional achievement, accomplished under the pressure of a military necessity.

ROMAN CAMP.

63. In the military history of Rome the camp has a degree of importance without a parallel in modern warfare. It was the soldier's home, a place of rest and security after the labours and dangers of the day; in it was the altar at which he worshipped. It was always fortified, even when intended for a single night. Indeed, it was like a fortified city, encompassed and protected by ramparts and a moat.

A Roman general seldom went into battle without a fortified camp directly in the rear. In modern warfare, those who are defeated in battle are exposed to all the perils of a disorderly retreat; a Roman army, on the contrary, after a defeat, retired in comparative safety to a well fortified camp.

64. In the Roman camp, each *legion, cohort*, and *maniple*, had a definite space assigned to it; and this space was bounded on all sides by a street of greater or less width. Each *maniple* occupied a rectangle 108 feet long and 48 feet wide, surrounded by a street, 12 feet wide. Accordingly, the entire space assigned to a *maniple*, including half the width of the streets which separated it from the adjacent *maniples*, was 120 feet long and 60 feet wide, as seen in the accompanying figure.

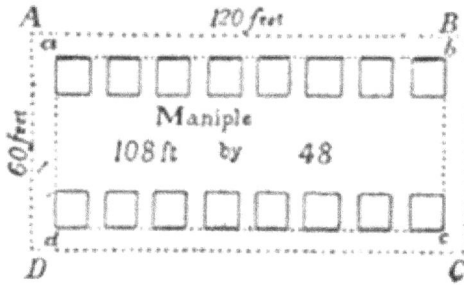

ABCD, the entire space assigned to a *maniple*, including half the street. abcd, the smaller rectangle, 108 feet long and 48 wide, actually occupied by the *maniple*. Along the side 'ab', in this last rectangle, were placed eight tents for the first century; and along the side 'dc' eight tents for the second century. The tents were 10 feet square, and were separated from each other by intervals of 4 feet.

The tents were covered with the skins of animals or with leather; hence the expression *sub pellibus*, in tents, in camp They were all placed with the front to the street; accordingly, the two rows faced in opposite directions. The beasts of burden were placed in the rear of the tents.

65. As a *cohort* contained three *maniples*, it would require for its accommodation three such rectangles as we have now described. Accordingly the space occupied by a *cohort* in camp was 180 feet long and 120 wide, as seen in the accompanying figure.

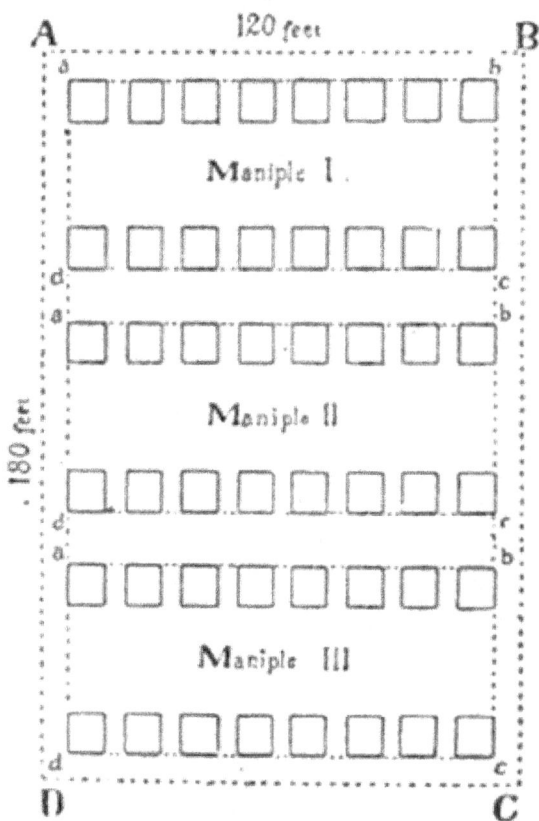

A _____ 120 feet _____ B

Maniple I.

Maniple II

Maniple III

180 feet

A B D C

Cohort in camp

ABCD, the space occupied by one *cohort* including one half the width of the streets which separate it from the other *cohorts*.

abcd the space occupied by each *maniple* for tents, arms, and beasts of burden.

In the arrangement of the three *maniples* of the *cohort*, the first was placed nearest to the wall of the camp.

66. Ten rectangles, 180 feet long and 120 feet wide, would furnish quarters for a *legion*; fifty such rectangles for five *legions*; but a camp for a Roman army must provide quarters not only for the *legions*, but also for the auxiliaries. The following plan, taken, with slight modifications, from Rüstow, shows the general arrangement of a Roman camp for an army consisting of five legions, with the usual force of auxiliaries:—

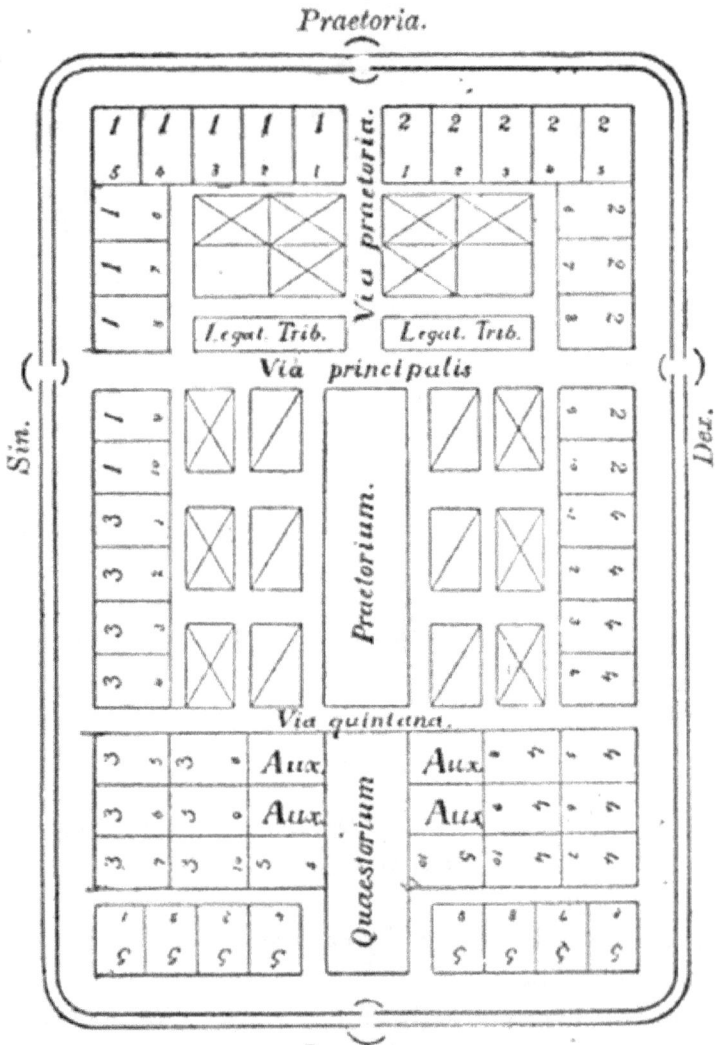

PLAN OF A ROMAN CAMP.
LENGTH, 2,100 FEET.
WIDTH, 1,400 FEET

The Roman camp was either a square, or a rectangle whose width was two-thirds of its length. The plan represents the latter form. The ancient authorities on the camp are Polybius, who lived in the second century, B.C., and a certain Hyginus, who, in the opinion of Marquardt, lived about the beginning of the third century, A.D.

The size of the camp must, of course, be adapted to the size of the army to be quartered in it. Rüstow gives the following formula to determine in feet the length and breadth of a camp for an army of any given size:

$$f = 200\sqrt{c} \text{ and } s = 1\frac{1}{2} \text{ times } f.$$

In which f equals the length of the *front*, c the number of cohorts in the army, and s the length of the side.

The camp represented in the plan is intended to accommodate five *legions*, or fifty *cohorts*. Here c = 50. Hence

$$f \text{ (the front)} = 206 \sqrt{50} = 200 \times 7 = 1,400 \text{ feet.}$$

$$s = 1\frac{1}{2} \text{ times } 1,400 = 2,100 \text{ feet.}$$

1. There were four gates, one in each side
   (1) the *Porta Praetoria*, in front, marked *Praetoria* in the plan;
   (2) the *Porta Decumana*, on the opposite side, marked *Decumana*;
   (3) the *Porta Principalis Dextra*, on the right side, marked *Dex.*; and
   (4) the *Porta Principalis Sinistra*, on the left side, marked *Sin.*
   Observe that the corners of the wall are rounded so as to be more easily defended.

2. *Legat. Trib.* = *Legati et Tribuni.*

3. *Aux.* = *Auxilia.*

4. The figure $\boxed{X}$ represents the space occupied by cavalry.

5. The figure $\boxed{/}$ the space occupied by the general and staff, except the lieutenants and *tribunes*, together with troops devoted to their personal service.

41

6. The figure ☐ the space occupied by the archers and slingers.

7. The rectangles with numerals represent the spaces occupied by the separate *cohorts*.

The upper numeral is the number of the legion; the lower numeral the number of the *cohort*. Thus $\boxed{\frac{2}{5}}$ represents the space occupied by the fifth *cohort* of the second *legion*.

67. When a battle was anticipated, the camp was placed with its front to the enemy; in other cases, it faced in the direction in which the army was marching. It was divided internally into three nearly equal parts by the two principal streets, both parallel to the front—the *Via Principalis* and the *Via Quintana*. The first or front part was called the *Praetentura*, the second or middle part the *Latera praetorii*, and the third *Retentura*. The *Via Praetoria*, another important street, led from the *Porta Praetoria* to the *Via Principalis*, dividing the *Praetentura* into two equal parts.

On a line with the *Via Praetoria* were situated:

(1), in the middle division of the camp, the *Praetorium*, the headquarters of the army, the *Praetorium* extended in length from the *Via Principalis* to the *Via Quintana*, and was from two hundred to three hundred feet wide. In it were the quarters of the general, the altars of the gods, and the tribunal, or judgment-seat, of the army.—and:

(2), in the *Retentura*, the *Quaestorium*,—the quarters of the *quaestor* and his staff. The *Quaestorium* furnished quarters, not only for the *quaestor* and his staff, but, also, for foreign ambassadors, and for hostages and prisoners. In it were also stored the supplies and the booty.

68. In the plan of the camp, observe:

(1) that between the wall and the tents was left an open space, probably from one hundred to two hundred feet wide, extending entirely around the camp, and:

(2) that the forces were distributed as follows:—

1. In the *Praetentura* were stationed (1), sixteen of

the fifty *cohorts*; (2), the lieutenants and *tribunes*; (3), one-half of all the cavalry; and (4), all the archers and slingers.

2. In the *Middle Division* of the camp, called *Latera, praetorii*, were stationed, besides the commander-in-chief, who occupied the *Praetorium* (1), twelve of the fifty *cohorts*; (2), one-half of all the cavalry; and (3), the entire staff of the commander-in-chief, except the lieutenants and the *tribunes*, together with the troops devoted to their personal service.

3. In the *Retentura* were stationed, in addition to the *quaestor* and his staff, (1) twenty-two of the fifty *cohorts*, and (2) the auxiliaries, except the cavalry, archers, and slingers. Observe in the internal arrangements of the camp that the auxiliaries, both cavalry and infantry, are stationed near the general and his staff, and that they are completely surrounded by the *legionary* soldiers.

69. In a camp intended for winter-quarters, wooden huts, thatched with straw, took the place of ordinary tents, and sheds were erected to protect the beasts of burden from wind and weather. Moreover, the space allowed to the different parts of the army was doubtless somewhat more ample than in a summer camp.

70. The fortifications of the camp consisted of a wall, *vallum*, and a ditch, or fosse, *fossa*. The wall seems to have been ordinarily about 6 feet high, and 6 or 8 feet broad at the top, the ditch about 9 feet wide at the top, and 7 feet deep. Vegetius, Book 1, 24, says that the ordinary ditch was either 9 feet wide and 7 feet deep, or 12 feet wide and 9 feet deep. In these dimensions, it has been observed that the width, as 9 or 12, is divisible by 3, and that the depth is obtained by adding one to 2 thirds of the width, as width 9, depth 2 thirds of $9 + 1 = 7$, or width 12, depth 2 thirds of $12 + 1 = 9$.

Rüstow infers that these instances are illustrations of a law, and that having the width of any ditch, we can thus at once obtain the depth. As a matter of fact, Caesar generally gives only the width.

In opposition to the view of Rüstow, Göler thinks that the normal depth of a ditch, whatever its width, was 9 feet, and that Caesar specifies the depth only when it does not conform to the ordinary standard. Doubtless, in fortifying a permanent camp, *castra stativa*, in a hostile country, the ditch was made wider and deeper, and the wall higher and broader. It has been observed that when Caesar gives the height of a wall with the width of the accompanying ditch, as ditch 9 feet wide, wall 6 feet high; ditch 15 feet wide, wall 10 feet high; ditch 18 feet wide, wall 12 feet high, the height of the wall is f of the width of the ditch.

This Rüstow believes to be the regular law. Indeed, some such relation as this between the dimensions of the ditch and the wall seems natural, as the earth thrown out of the former was used in constructing the latter. It was sometimes surmounted with a breastwork of palisades, *lorica*,

The breastwork was usually made by driving green stakes into the ground, and by binding them firmly together by intertwining their branches. The general height of the breastwork was four or five feet, but in some instances pinnacles, *pinnae*, projected above it two or three feet, as seen in the figure in 71, and in special cases wooden towers were erected on it at convenient intervals.

Each gate was probably 40 feet wide, and was defended within and without either by a transverse or by a tambour, as seen in the above plan. The Gauls and the Germans fortified their camps, not by permanent works like the Romans, but by arranging their chariots and wagons in a circle, and using them as a rampart. After a defeat, they often retreated to these temporary defences.

71. The following figure represents a vertical section of a wall and ditch, the former surmounted with a breastwork of palisades:—

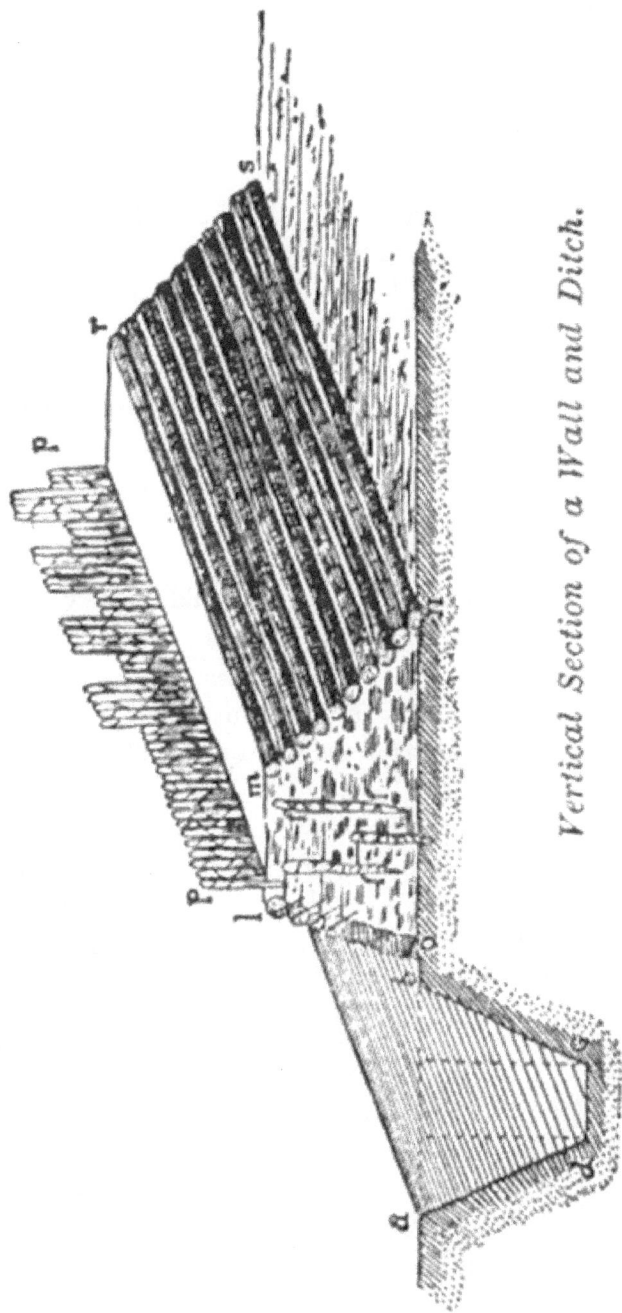

Vertical Section of a Wall and Ditch.

abed represents a ditch, *fossa fastigata*, 9 feet wide and 7 feet deep. lmno, a wall or rampart, *vallum*, 6 feet high, and 6 feet wide at the top, furnished with steps on the inside, *i.e.*, on the side 'mrsn.'
pp, palisades.

ff, fascines imbedded in the work, to strengthen it.

72. The side of the ditch nearest to the wall is called the *scarp*, and the opposite side, the *counterscarp*. A ditch with sloping sides, as in the figure, was called *fossa fastigata*; with vertical sides, *fossa directis lateribus*, and with sloping scarp but vertical counterscarp, *fossa punica*. The first form was generally used by Caesar, though the second also occurs.

73. The wall was constructed largely from the earth and stone taken from the ditch, but to give the structure greater firmness and strength, branches of trees, bushes, stakes, and fascines were imbedded in it. When the sides of the wall were quite steep, they were usually covered with sods or with brush in the form of fascines. Sometimes logs were used for the same purpose. Moreover, these logs and fascines could be arranged in steps, so that from within the bank or wall could be easily ascended. See figure in **71**. The selection of the place for the camp was a duty which required skill, judgment, and experience.

It was of vital importance that the camp should be pitched, if possible, on a gently sloping hillside of sufficient extent, within easy reach of a good supply of wood and water. It was also important that it should not be near any hill from which an enemy could reconnoitre it, or near any dense forest in which he could be concealed.

Accordingly, this important trust was generally committed to a *tribune*, or to some other officer of the staff, at the head of a detachment of *centurions* and *legionaries*. They marched in advance of the main body of the army, under the protection of the van-guard, and were expected to have the outlines of the camp well defined on the arrival of the *legions*.

74. For Roman soldiers, marching through a hostile country, no small part of each day's work was the fortification of the camp, but they shrunk from no labour, and were scarcely less expert with the pick and the spade than with the spear and the sword. With such labourers, three or four hours, in the judgment of Rüstow, would be ample for the complete fortification of the camp.

75. But Roman camps in a hostile country were not only strongly fortified, but also carefully guarded. In cases requiring only ordinary vigilance, the duty of keeping guard during the night-watches was entrusted to five *cohorts* detailed for the purpose from different *legions*.

The tattoo, the signal for setting the night-watches, was sounded at nightfall. A *cohort* was stationed at each gate, and sentinels were posted on every part of the wall. A fifth *cohort* was detailed for guard duty in the quarters of the general and *quaestor*, while every *cohort* had its own sentry. In cases of unusual peril, the guard was greatly strengthened; sometimes two or three *cohorts* guarded each gate.

As the night was divided into four equal watches, the guard was divided into four reliefs, each one of which was on duty during one-fourth of the night. The three reliefs not on duty slept upon their arms, as a sort of picket-guard.

76. The reveille was sounded at daybreak. If the march was to be resumed, three successive signals were sounded. At the first signal, the tents were struck; at the second, the beasts of burden received their loads; and at the third, the column moved. If, however, a battle was imminent, the march was not resumed; the tents were left standing, and the camp was committed to the care of a strong guard.

This guard sometimes consisted of four or five *cohorts*, detailed from separate *legions*, and sometimes of one or more legions recently enrolled. Then the soldiers, disencumbered of their knapsacks, and armed and equipped for action, truly *expediti*, marched out of the camp, and were at once marshalled in line of battle.

77. Roman generals made it an unfailing rule to take every possible advantage of position. For them an open plain was not a good battlefield. The Roman mode of attack required an elevated position, from which the heavy javelins could be hurled into the ranks of the enemy with the greatest effect. We see how very important it was that the camp should be pitched upon a hillside of sufficient extent to enable the general to marshal his army for battle near his camp, if not in front of it.

Military Standards and Martial Music.

78. The general standard of the army was the banner, *vexillum*, of the commander-in-chief. When displayed from the general's tent in the *Praetorium*, it was a signal to prepare for immediate action, and when waved before the legions advancing in order of battle, it was the signal for the charge, *incursus*. It contained the name of the general and of the army, inscribed in large red letters on a white ground.

79. Each legion had its own standard, which was entrusted to the special care of the chief centurion, the *primipilus* of the legion. The loss of a standard was a calamity and a disgrace, both, to the standard-bearer and to the *legion*. It was an eagle of the size of a dove, generally of silver, though under the empire sometimes of gold. The eagle was represented with uplifted wings, as seen in plate 1, 9. Sometimes a small banner, *vexillum*, on which was embroidered the number of the *legion*, was placed directly below the eagle.

80. The ten *cohorts* of the *legion* had their special standards, *signa*, the general name for a standard was *signum*, and for a standard-bearer *signifer*, but the more specific names *aquila* and *aquilifer* were generally used to designate the standard and the standard-bearer of the *legion*. The bravest and strongest soldiers were selected as standard-bearers. See *signiferi* in plate 2, 5.

Göler thinks that the *maniples* had standards, and that the standard of the first *maniple* was also the standard of the entire *cohort*, but Rüstow rejects this view as utterly untenable which were of various forms, sometimes very simple and sometimes more elaborate.

A standard was sometimes simply the figure of an open hand upon a staff, and sometimes the figure of an animal, as a wolf or an ox. For specimens of the latter, see plate 1, 5.

81. The standards carried by the cavalry, by the light-armed infantry, and by detachments detailed for special service, were simple banners, *vexilla*. For the general appearance, form, and size of the *vexilla*, see plate 1, 5, and plate 2, 8. Observe in plate 2, 5, that one of the elaborate standards has a *vexillum* at the top.

82. The chief musical instrument in a Roman army, and indeed the only one mentioned in the Commentaries on the Gallic war, was the trumpet, tuba, Göler thinks that every century had at least one tuba. This was a wind instrument of brass in the form of a modern trumpet. The only musicians mentioned by Caesar, in either of his works are the *tubicines* and the *bucinatores*, both of whom are represented with their instruments in plate 2, 6 and 7; but the *lituus*, a modification of the trumpet, curved near the end was doubtless used in the cavalry.

It seems probable that the *bucinator* used not only the *bucina*, but also the *cornu*, the horn, a wind instrument made generally from the horn of a wild ox, and furnished with a silver mouthpiece, but sometimes made from brass.

According to Göler, the various military evolutions were first signalled by the horn, and then proclaimed throughout the army by the trumpet. The *classicum*, which, on the field of battle, was the signal for the charge, was made by the united blasts of the horn and the trumpet. Lucan, *Pharsalia*, I., 237, characterizes the notes of the *lituus* and the *tuba* in these words: *stridor lituum clangorque tubarum*.

ROMAN MODE OF ATTACK.

83. When the Roman general had secured his favourite position on the gentle declivities of a range of hills with the enemy sufficiently near in the plain below, he ordered the signal to be sounded with the trumpet. The *legions* advanced slowly and steadily in order of battle until they were within five hundred or six hundred feet of the enemy, when the standard of the commander-in-chief was displayed, and the united blasts of the horn and the trumpet sounded the signal for the charge. From this point, the *legions*, with poised javelins in their front ranks, *pilis infestis*, advanced upon the run until the hostile lines were within forty or fifty feet of each other, when a salvo of javelins from the front of the *legions* carried consternation and death into the ranks of the opposing *phalanx*.

The *pila* which penetrated the hostile shields often stuck fast in them, thus rendering the men unfit for action. Sometimes three or more shields in the dense *phalanx* were pinned together by these weapons. Then, with drawn swords, the Roman soldiers charged the broken ranks of the foe. This onset of the Roman legions with *pilum* and sword has been compared to a volley of musketry, instantly followed by a bayonet-charge.

It is not probable that all the men in the front rank charged with the sword at the same time, as they stood too close together in rank and file to allow the free use of that weapon. Rüstow conjectures that the odd numbers in the front rank sprang forward, while the even numbers kept their places in the line, and that thus each man secured ample room for the charge.

84. Thus all along the front line a deadly conflict was waged hand to hand,—a series of duels, as Rüstow expresses it. In this account of the Roman mode of attack, we have followed Rüstow. For the moment, it was of course impossible to preserve unbroken ranks in the front of the *cohorts* thus engaged. Along the front line, the whole of the first century of each *maniple* participated, either directly or indirectly, in the terrible struggle.

While the first two ranks bore the brunt of the battle, the other three, as opportunity offered, hurled their javelins over the heads of the combatants into the hostile ranks in the rear, and held themselves in readiness to rush to the relief of their companions in case of need. Meanwhile, the second century of each *maniple*, remaining firm and immovable, gave stability to the line.

85. Thus far the *cohorts* of the second line had taken no part in the battle; but soon they, too, were seen to be in motion, and, advancing quickly in battle-array through the intervals of the first line, they hurled their javelins into the ranks of the bewildered foe, and then with drawn swords rushed into the thickest of the fight.

The exhausted *cohorts*, thus timely relieved, retired to reform their shattered line, and to recover breath and strength for a new onset. Thus the first and second lines continued the conflict, alternately relieving each other, until the enemy, exhausted and demoralized, yielded to the repeated onsets of the Roman cohorts.

In the opinion of Rüstow, a line of Roman *cohorts* seldom remained in active conflict more than fifteen minutes at a time. The third line formed the reserve, and was summoned to the front only in cases of special need.

The Gallic mode of conducting a battle was wholly unlike the Roman. The Gauls staked the issue largely on the first onset. Raising their fearful battle-cry, they advanced against the enemy in solid *phalanx*, and strove to overwhelm him by the mere momentum and weight of moving masses.

The unit in the German line of battle was the solid wedge, the *cuneus*, so celebrated in the early history of Germany. The different tribes were massed separately. The charge on the field of battle was an impetuous onset in masses.

Roman Method of Taking Fortified Places.

86. The Romans recognized three different methods of taking fortified places:—

1. By Storm, Assault—*oppugnatio repentina.*

2. By Investment, Blockade—*obsidio.*

3. By Siege, with active operations—*oppugnatio operibus.*

87. In attacking fortified towns, the Romans often employed certain engines which corresponded to artillery in modern warfare. They were designated by the general name *tormenta*, from *torqueo*, to twist, as their motive power was derived from the torsion of firmly twisted ropes; but they were of several varieties.

1. The Scorpion—*scorpio*—was a large cross-bow, resting on a standard, as seen in the accompanying figure.

51

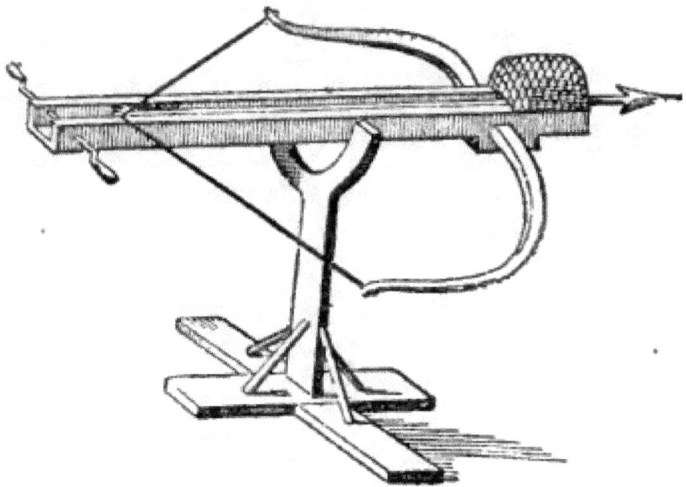

Scorpion.

2. The Catapult—*catapulta*—was an engine for hurling heavy javelins or other missiles. This was also a modification of the cross-bow; but the arms of the bow were straight sticks of timber, and its elasticity, or its power of recoil, was produced by the torsion of a large rope, or cable, made from hair or sinews twisted to the greatest possible tension.

Only the very strongest hair was used for this purpose; and Jähns suggests that it was probably subjected to a special process to increase its strength. The sinews and tendons from the necks of bulls and from the legs of goats, were especially prized for this purpose. The construction of the catapult, and the mode of working it, are seen in the following figure:—

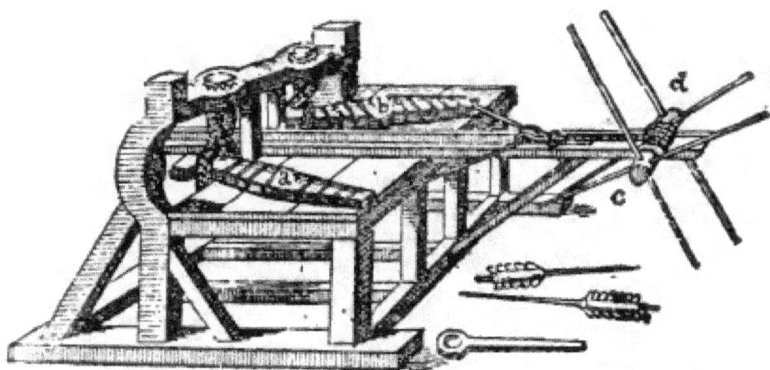

Catapult.

Observe that the two sticks of timber, 'a' and 'b', are inserted in two large ropes, or cables, and that their ends, like the ends of a bow, are connected together by a strong cord. In working the catapult, the middle of this cord was drawn back by means of a windlass, 'cd.' Practically, therefore, the catapult was a bow of immense power.

3. The *Ballista* was an engine for hurling balls, stones, and even heavy sticks of wood. In principle the motive power was the same as in the catapult, from which it differed mainly in the fact that it hurled missiles at an angle of 45 degrees. For the mode of working the *ballista* see figure 5 in the foreground of plate 5.

According to Rustow und Kochly, *Geschiclite des grie-chischen Kriegswesens*, the ballista had such remarkable projectile force that it threw heavy, missiles, on an average, a quarter of a mile, and that it sometimes reached twice that distance. In the *Commentaries on the Civil War*, Caesar tells us that beams, or poles, 12 feet long, pointed with iron, hurled from *ballistae*, passed through four rows of hurdles, probably in the form of *vineae* (**90**), or *plutei* (**92**), and planted themselves in the earth.

The *ballista* is sometimes compared to the modern mortar. It was capable of throwing missiles of great weight. Stones weighing from one hundred to one hundred and thirty pounds were at times hurled by it. See Rüstow and Köchly; also Schambach, *Geschutzverwendung bei den Römern.*

4. The *Onager* was a modification of the catapult. It had only one arm, and that arm worked vertically, while the arms of the catapult worked horizontally. See figure 4 in the foreground of plate 5. Observe that the arm is drawn down by means of a windlass, and that it flies back with great violence as soon as it is released.

88. The *Turris ambulatoria* was a movable tower, often used by the Romans in attacking fortified cities. It was, of course, of various sizes; but ordinarily it consisted of ten stories, and was about ninety feet high, twenty-five feet square at the base and twenty at the top. Each story had an outer gallery, extending entirely around it. Athenaeus, the author of a work, written, probably, about 200 B. C., περὶ Μηχανημάτων, mentions a tower 180 feet high and 35 feet square at the base. See plate 5, 1

89. The tower, which was moved forward by means of rollers worked from within, was supplied with one or more drawbridges, which, on being let down upon the wall, furnished the attacking party a passage to the enemy's works. The lower story was usually supplied with a battering-ram; while the upper stories were occupied with the engines of war—the *tormenta.* The *turris ambulatoria*, armed with the battering-ram and the *tormenta*, and well supplied with archers and slingers, was a movable battery of great power.

90. The *Vinea*, used to protect soldiers and workmen during siege operations, was a movable shed or arbour, resting on rollers. According to Vegetius, it was usually 16 feet long, 7 wide, and 8 high. The roof was of timber, or thick plank, supported by upright posts; the sides were of strong wicker-work. It was sometimes entirely open at both ends, and sometimes partially closed. The roof and sides were covered with raw hides, as a protection against fire.

91. The *Musculus* was a variety of the *vinea*. It was of smaller

Vinea.

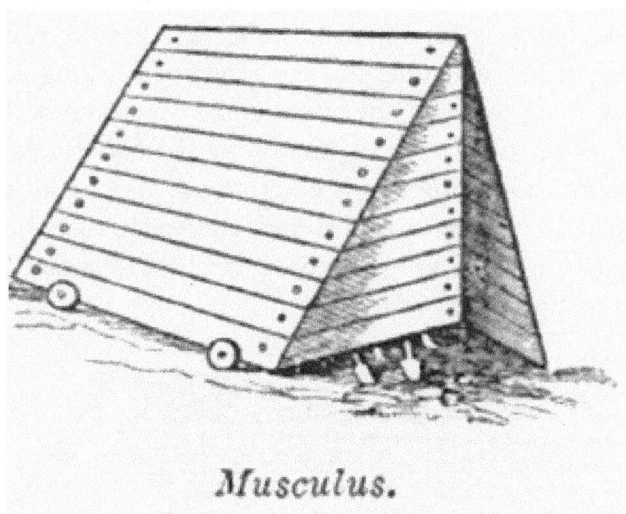

Musculus.

size than the ordinary *vinea*, but of much greater strength, as it was intended to be used in the immediate vicinity of the enemy's works, especially to protect sappers and miners in undermining the wall. Caesar, in his *Commentaries on the Civil War*, Book II., 10, has described the kind of *musculus* which he used in the siege of Massilia. It was so strong that blocks of stone hurled from the top of the wall fell harmless upon it. The roof was made of sticks of timber two feet thick, overlaid with brick and mortar, covered with raw hides. See the accompanying figure.

92. The *Pluteus* was a movable breastwork, or screen, resting on rollers. It was usually seven or eight feet in height, and was supplied with loop-holes, through which archers could discharge their arrows. It was of various .forms, as seen in figures 1, 2, and 3.

93. The *Testudo arietaria*, also used in storming cities, consisted of a movable shed, like a *vinea*, in which was suspended a battering-ram (*aries*), in the form of a heavy stick of timber, from sixty to a hundred feet long, armed with a large head of bronze or iron. It was worked by men under the cover of the *testudo*, and was used to effect a breach in the wall. For the general appearance of this machine, and the mode of working it, see the *testudo arietaria* battering the tower in the background of plate 5. Caesar seems to have made little use of the battering-ram. The Gallic walls, according to his description, were so substantially constructed, of large beams, stones, and earth, that they could not be destroyed either by fire or by the battering-ram. The following figure is from Göler:

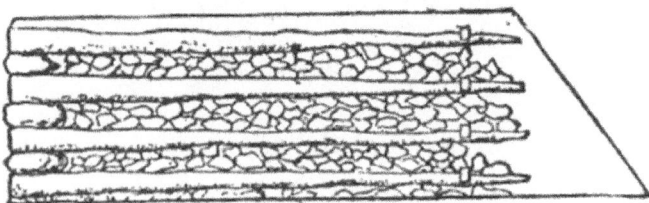

Vertical Section of Gallic Wall.

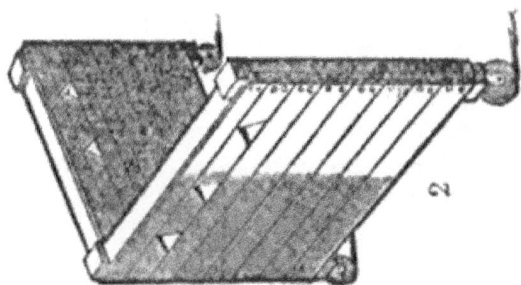

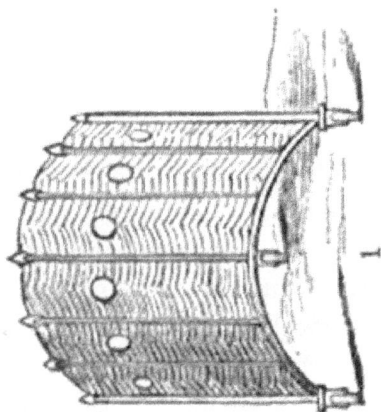

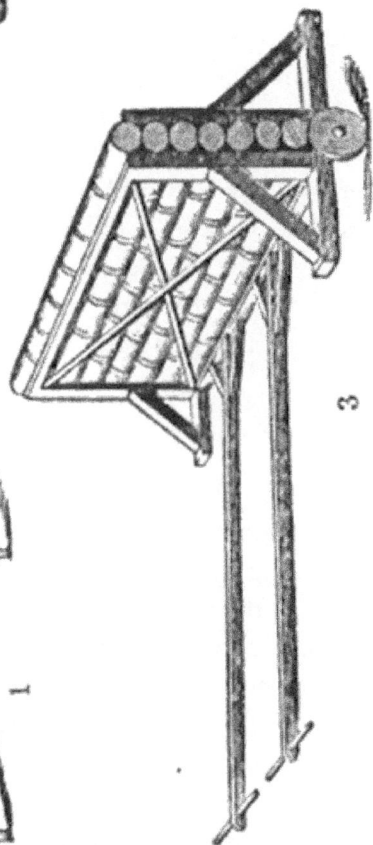

Plutei.

THE STORMING OF CITIES—*OPPUGNATIO REPENTINA*.

94. This method of attack was usually adopted when there was a reasonable prospect of immediate success without great loss, especially in proceeding against cities which were well supplied with provisions, but were neither strongly garrisoned nor defended by formidable works.

95. Aided by his engines of war, a Roman general who could lead veteran *legions* to the attack sometimes found the capture of a walled town a comparatively easy task.

96. Archers and slingers, protected by *plutei*, and sharpshooters with *catapults* and *ballistae*, drove the enemy from his works. Some filled the moat, while others, under the cover of *musculi*, strove to undermine the wall, or to set fire to the gates; the tower was moved slowly forward, the battering-ram began its work; numerous storming columns, forming the *testudo*, with their shields close-locked over their heads, as seen in plate 5, advanced to the attack; the ladders were quickly applied; the sharpshooters, archers, and slingers, redoubled their efforts; the walls were scaled; the gates were thrown open, and the legions entered.

INVESTMENT, BLOCKADE OF CITIES—*OBSIDIO*

97. The Romans sometimes compelled hostile cities to surrender, by enclosing them so completely within a continuous line of strong fortifications, that neither supplies nor succour could reach them. This plan was adopted when the place was too strongly fortified and too strongly garrisoned to be taken by storm, especially if the population was large, and the supply of provisions limited. To ensure success, it was sometimes necessary to construct a second line of works at a suitable distance from the first, and outside of the investing army, as a precaution against attack from without, in case any attempt should be made to relieve the city.

The most remarkable instance mentioned in the *Commentaries* of this method of taking fortified towns, was the investment

ab, *Pinnae.*
bc, *Lorica,* consisting of *plutei.*

Section of Caesar's Contravallation at Alesia.

of Alesia. The town was garrisoned by a force of 80,000 Gauls; Caesar invested it, and for forty days he lay intrenched before it between two concentric lines of almost impregnable works; a mighty array of confederate Gauls, 250,000 strong, arrived in the rear of his intrenchments; but Roman valour triumphed, and Alesia surrendered to the conqueror.

98. The works with which Caesar enclosed this stronghold of the Gauls were in some respects among the most remarkable mentioned in Roman history. The figure on the preceding page, from Napoleon and Göler, represents a vertical section of the inner line of works, called in modern phraseology, contravallation. In modern phraseology, the inner line, or that which invests the city, is called contravallation, that outside of the investing army, circumvallation.

This line of works was 11 Roman miles in length, and 400 feet in width. Observe that on the side toward the city was a ditch 20 feet wide; that on the opposite side, 400 feet from this ditch, was a rampart 12 feet high, and that between these two points were arranged (1) two ditches, each 15 feet wide; (2) five rows of trunks of trees, with branches sharpened to a point, so planted in the earth that only the branches were in sight, called *cippi*; (3) eight rows of small pits 3 feet deep, each with a sharpened stake firmly set in its centre, called *lilia*, lilies, and (4) an indefinite number of short stakes entirely sunk in the earth, to which iron hooks were attached, called *stimuli*, spurs.

SIEGE OF FORTIFIED PLACES—*OPPUGNATIO OPERIBUS.*

99. With the Romans, a formal siege involved, not only the use of all the ordinary engines of war, but also the long and tedious labour of constructing an *agger*. It was resorted to only in difficult cases, when a simple investment would be inadequate and when a direct assault without special preparation would promise little success.

The *agger* was a mound, or rampart, beginning several hundred feet from the wall of the besieged city, and extending directly toward it, until it finally reached and overtopped it, and thus furnished a broad highway, on which a storming column could advance directly to the highest part of the enemy's works. In some cases the *agger* did not reach the top of the wall, but was surmounted by one or more towers, which, on being moved up to the enemy's works, secured the necessary height for the storming party.

100. An *agger* of the ordinary dimensions, 400 or 500 feet long, 50 or 60 feet wide, and from 50 to 80 feet high,—the agger at Avaricum was 80 feet high—required for its construction an enormous amount of timber, stones, earth, and brush. The trunks of trees from 20 to 40 feet in length, and from 1 to 2 feet in thickness, were of the first importance; indeed the words of Lucan must have been at times almost literally true:—

"*Procumbunt nemora et spoliantur robore silvae.*"
—Lucan's *Pharsalia*. III.,

101. To aid the learner in understanding the more important steps in a formal siege, we add the following illustrations. (See following page). Fig. 1, Ground Plan of Siege Operations:—

1. ABCD represents the enemy's wall.

2. abcd, the space to be occupied by the *agger*.

3. mm, *musculi*, protecting labourers levelling the ground.

4. VV, the line of *vineae*, forming a covered way through which materials were brought for the *agger*.

5. PP, a line of *plutei*, protecting the men while building the first section of the *agger*.

6. TT, *turres ambulatoriae*, armed with *tormenta*, and supplied with archers and slingers.

7. pppp, a continuous line of *plutei*, nearly parallel to the enemy's wall, protecting archers and slingers.

8. vv, vv, two lines of *vineae*, parallel to the *agger*, forming each a covered way by which soldiers passed to the towers and to the lines of *plutei*. The line of *plutei*, parallel to the enemy's works, and the lines of *vineae* leading to it, are

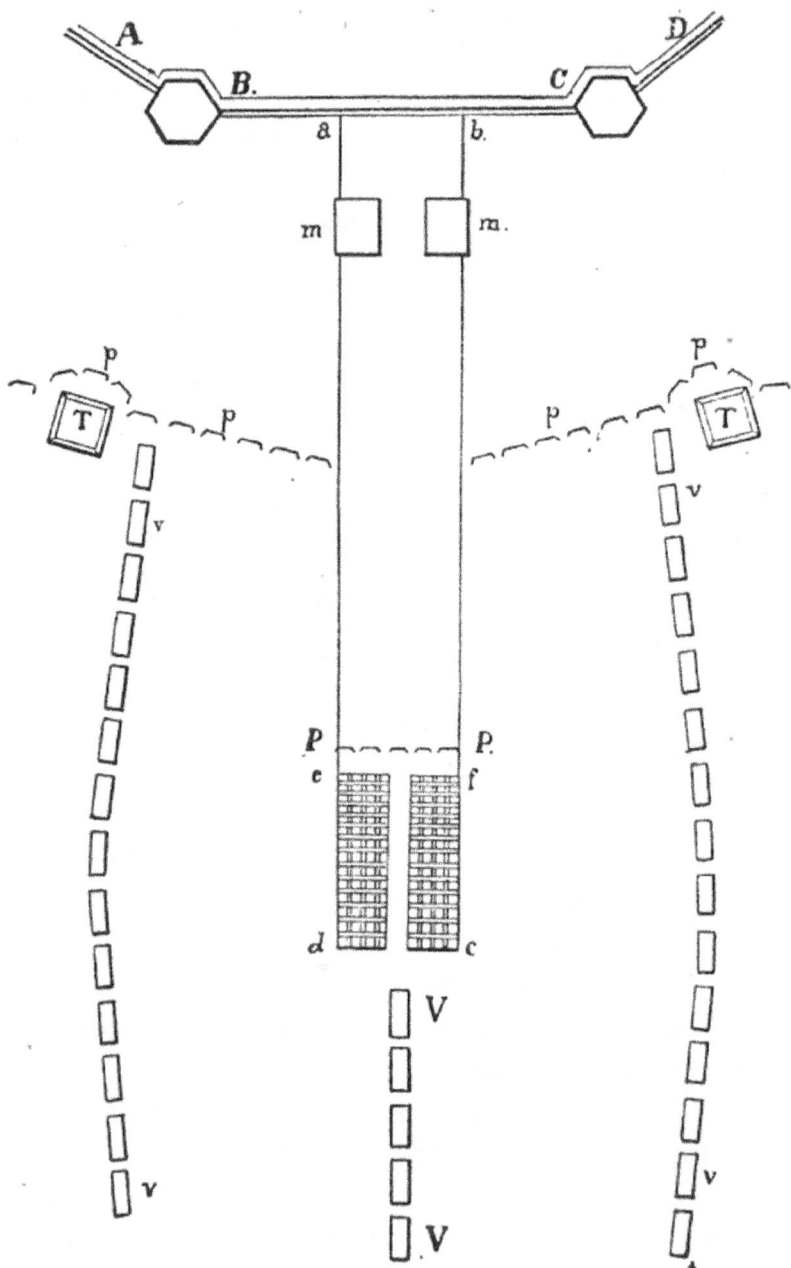

Figure 1.   Ground Plan of Siege Operations.

sometimes compared to the parallels and approaches in modern warfare.

9. cdef, a horizontal section of a part of the first story of the *agger*, showing how the logs were arranged, with intervals between them, and in layers at right angles with each other, showing also an open gallery or way through the middle.

102. An *agger*, 80 feet in height, usually consisted of eight or ten stories. On each floor was an open gallery, or hall, 10 or 12 feet wide and 8 or 10 feet high, extending the whole length of the *agger*. The work of construction began at a distance of 400 or 500 feet from the enemy's wall, from which most of its defenders had been driven by the archers and slingers behind the line of *plutei*, and by the artillerymen in the towers. The materials were brought through the covered way formed by the line of *vineae* 'VV,' while those who were engaged in the actual work of construction were protected by the *plutei*, 'PP.' First, large logs were placed firmly upon the ground parallel to each other and at suitable intervals; upon these was placed a second layer of logs at right angles with them, as seen in figure 1.

The open spaces between the logs were then filled with earth, stones, sods, brush, etc. Through the middle was left a passage, or open gallery, 10 or 12 feet wide, as stated above. The work continued in this way until the sides reached the height of 8 or 10 feet, when the open passage was covered overhead with a layer of timbers placed across it. Thus was finished the first section of the first story of the *agger*.

103. The *plutei*, 'PP,' were next moved forward 30 or 40 feet, and under their protection the second section of the first story was constructed in the same style and manner as the first section. The timber and other materials were brought first through the *vineae*, 'VV,' and then through the covered gallery in the first section. A line of *plutei*, 'P,' as seen in figure 2, was then placed across the front of the second floor, and the building of the first section of the second story was begun. The materials were all brought

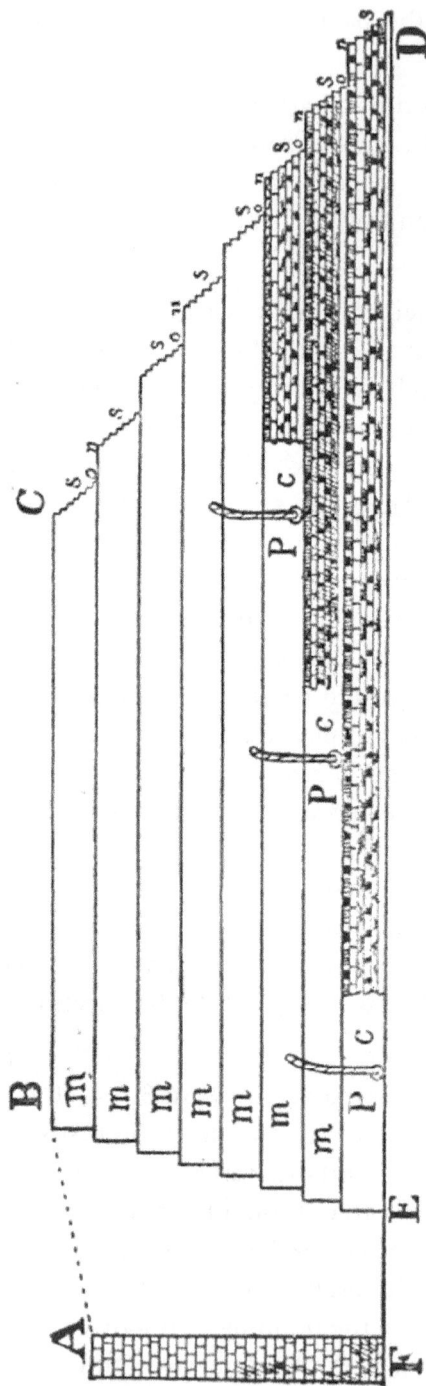

Figure 2. *Vertical Section of an Agger in Process of Construction.*

1. AF, represents the enemy's wall.
2. ABCDEF, section of the entire agger.
3. BCDE, part that may be regularly constructed.
4. ABEF, part especially exposed to the enemy's missiles, to be filled at last as best it may.
5. cs, part already constructed on the first, second, and third floors.
6. ms, a story with gallery, or hall, through its whole length.
7. s, stairs leading from one floor to another.
8. on, landing at the top of the stairs.
9. P, a line of *plutei* protecting the men at work.

through the *vineae* and up the stairs, 's,' to the landing, 'on,' which was a platform extending the whole width of the *agger*, thus affording easy access to the gallery, or hall, on the second floor.

104. As soon as the second section of the first story was finished, the *plutei* were again moved forward, and the third section was begun. At the same time, the *plutei* on the second floor, 'P,' in figure 2, were moved forward, and the second section of the second story was begun. *Plutei*, 'P,' were then placed on the third floor, and the first section of the third story was begun. This, like the second, was reached by stairs, leading to the landing, which furnished access to the hall, or passage, on this floor.

105. Thus the construction of the *agger* went on; one section after another was added, one story after another, until BCDE was finished. The enemy often attempted to prevent the completion of the *agger*, either by setting it on fire, or by undermining it; but, if he failed in this, he ordinarily lost courage, and surrendered before the completion of the works. Thus the *Aduatuci* surrendered when they saw the tower approaching the wall. The part nearest to the enemy, ABEF, still remained to be filled as best it might.

Then through all the halls on the different floors were brought logs, stones, brush, fascines, sods, and the like, and were hurled into one confused mass, until the space was filled. The top of the heap was next hastily levelled off and made passable. The decisive moment, for which all this elaborate preparation had been made, had at length arrived. The archers and slingers redoubled their efforts, and the heavy artillery swept the walls with its missiles, as the storming column advanced over the *agger*, and planted the Roman eagle upon the enemy's works.

Ships of War—*Naves Longae*.

106. Caesar had no organized navy during his Gallic campaigns, but he built ships as occasion required, and manned them with his legionary soldiers. Rowers and sailors could be readily obtained. His veteran legions could fight either on land or sea.

107. The Roman ships of war were seven or eight times as long as they were wide, and were accordingly called *naves longae*, in distinction from the transports, *naves onerariae*, which were much shorter in proportion to their width. They were armed in front with a formidable beak (*rostrum*), with which they often pierced and sunk the enemy's ships. The *naves onerariae* were transports, or ships of burden. They were four times as long as they were wide; they were propelled chiefly by means of sails, although supplied with oars to be used in case of need. Though provided with sails, they were propelled chiefly by oars. They carried the usual engines of war, the *tormenta*, were furnished with grappling-irons, and sometimes had towers on their decks.

The most important varieties were the *triremes,* with three banks of oars, and the *quinqueremes*, with five banks. See plate 6. According to *Graser*, a *trireme* was 149 feet long, with a deck 18 feet wide, and carried 232 tons burden. Without the use of sails, it had 24 horse-power, and its rate of speed was 10 knots an hour. The oars were arranged in tiers or banks, those in the upper bank being 13½ feet long, those in the middle bank 10½, and those in the lower bank 7½.

The regular complement of men for a *trireme* seems to have been 225, of whom 31 were officers and soldiers, 20 sailors, and 174 rowers; for a *quinquereme*, 375, of whom 310 were rowers; but we learn on the authority of Polybius that the Romans increased the number of soldiers, and that the *quinqueremes* in the Punic wars generally had each 120 soldiers on board.

The *naves actuariae* and the *naves speculatoriae*, also called *specula'.oria naviyia*, were small light vessels constructed for speed.

PLATE 1.

1. Funditor. 2. Levis Armaturae Pedites. 3. Legionarii Milites.
4. Sarcijnae. 5. Equites.

PLATE 2.

1. IMPERATOR. 2. LEGATUS. 3. CENTURIO. 4. LICTOR. 5. SIGNIFERI.
6. BUCINATOR. 7. TUBICEN. 8. VEXILLUM. 9. AQUILA.

PLATE 3.

1. MATERIA AND CASTRA MUNIENDA COMPORTATUR. 2. CAPTIVI.

PLATE 4

GALLI, 1. EQUES. 2. PEDES. 3. SIGNIFER. 4. DUX.

Plate 5. 1. Turris ambulatoria. 2. Testudo Arietaria. 3. Testudo. 4. Onager. 5. Ballista. 6.

PLATE 7. VICTORY OVER THE HELVETII. 1. 24—27

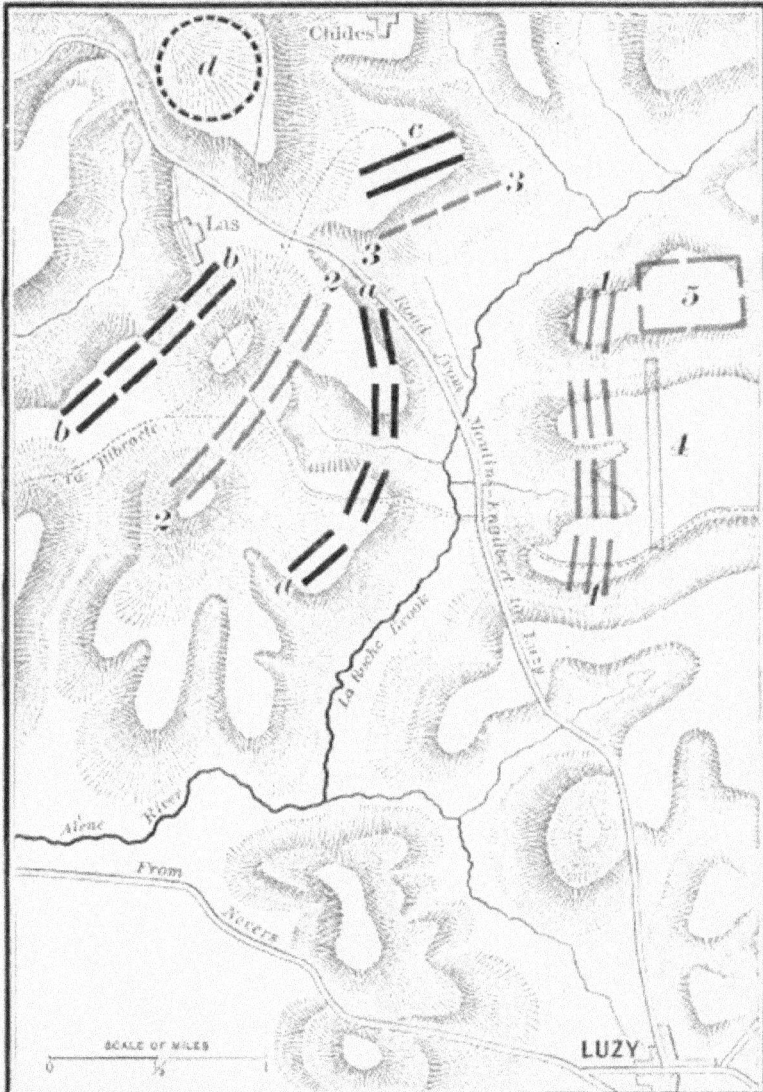

EXPLANATION.

1. Romans in line of battle with the *Helvetii* (*a, a*) in front of them.
2. The first two of the Roman lines after they had driven back the Helvetii (*b, b*) to the neighboring hill.
3. The third line with the *Boii* and *Tulingi* (*c*) in front of it.
4. Two new legions with auxiliaries. 5. Roman camp.
a. Helvetii, first position. *b. Helvetii,* second position. *c. Boii* and *Tulingi.*
d. Helvetian camp defended by wagons, chariots and baggage.
———————— *Romans.* ———————— *Helvetii.*

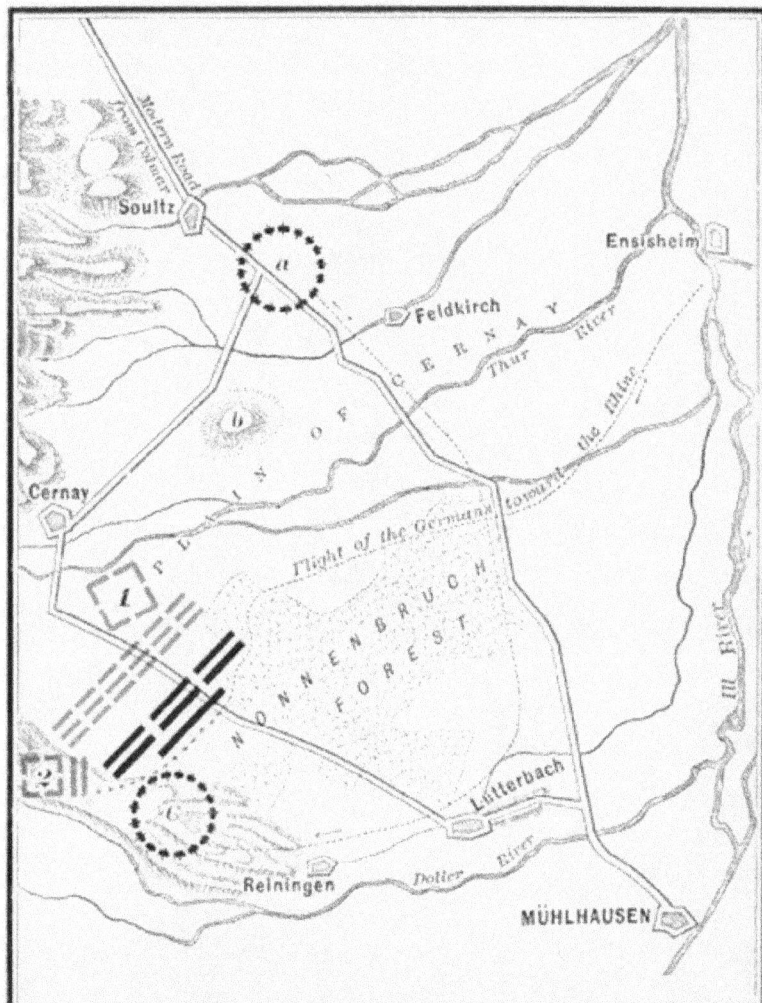

PLATE 8. VICTORY OVER ARIOVISTUS. 1. 42—51.

EXPLANATION.

1. Caesar's large camp.

2. Caesar's small camp.

a. First camp of Ariovistus.

b. Hill on which Caesar and Ariovistus met.

c. Second camp of Ariovistus.

———— *Romans.* ————*Germans.*

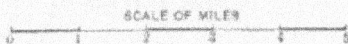

SCALE OF MILES

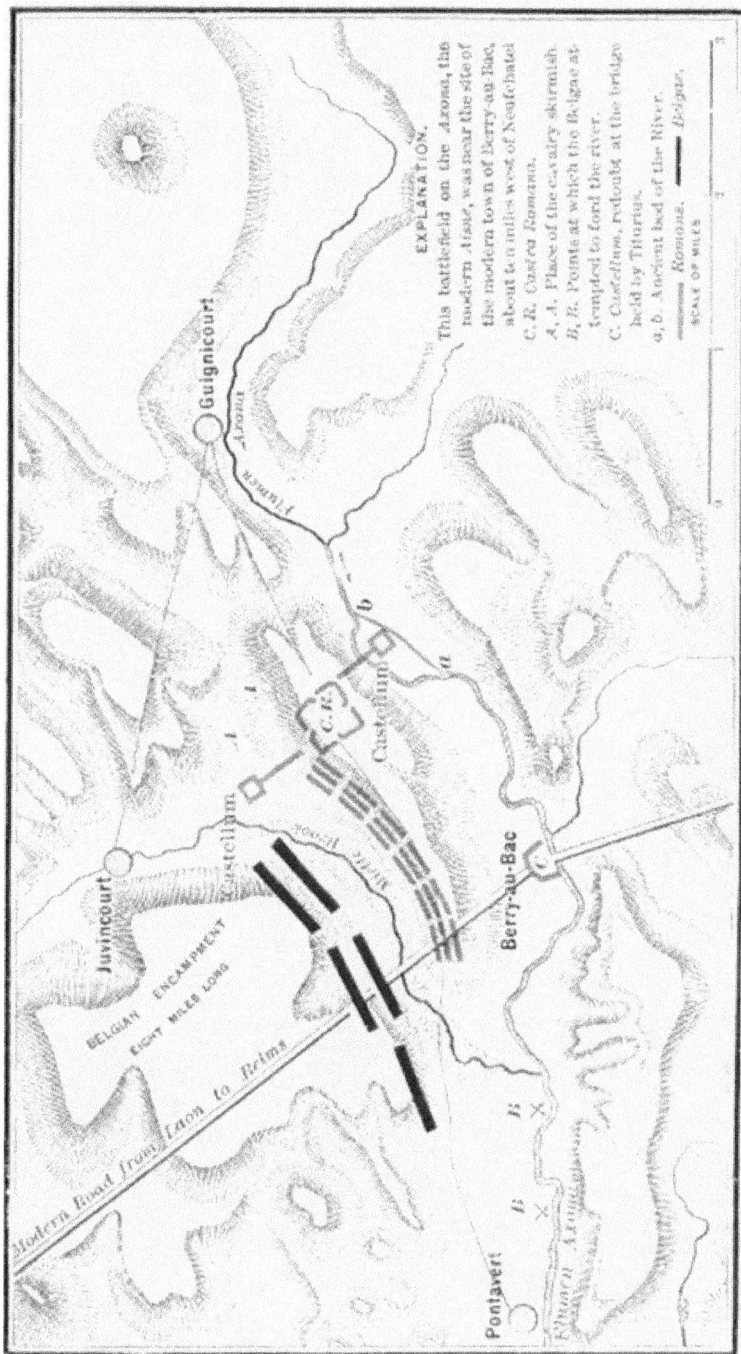

PLATE 9. BATTLE OF THE AXIONA. 2 6—10

EXPLANATION.

This battlefield on the Axona, the modern Aisne, was near the site of the modern town of Berry-au-Bac, about ten miles west of Neufchatel

C. R. Castra Romana.

A. A. Place of the cavalry skirmish.

B, B. Point at which the Belgae attempted to ford the river.

C. Castellum, redoubt at the bridge held by Titurius.

a, b. Ancient bed of the River.

Romans. ━━━━━━━ Belgae.

SCALE OF MILES

Guignicourt

Axona

Flumen

Juvincourt

Castellum

Castellum

C. R.

Berry-au-Bac

BELGIAN ENCAMPMENT EIGHT MILES LONG

North Bank

Modern Road from Laon to Reims

Pontavert

B

B

Flumen Axona

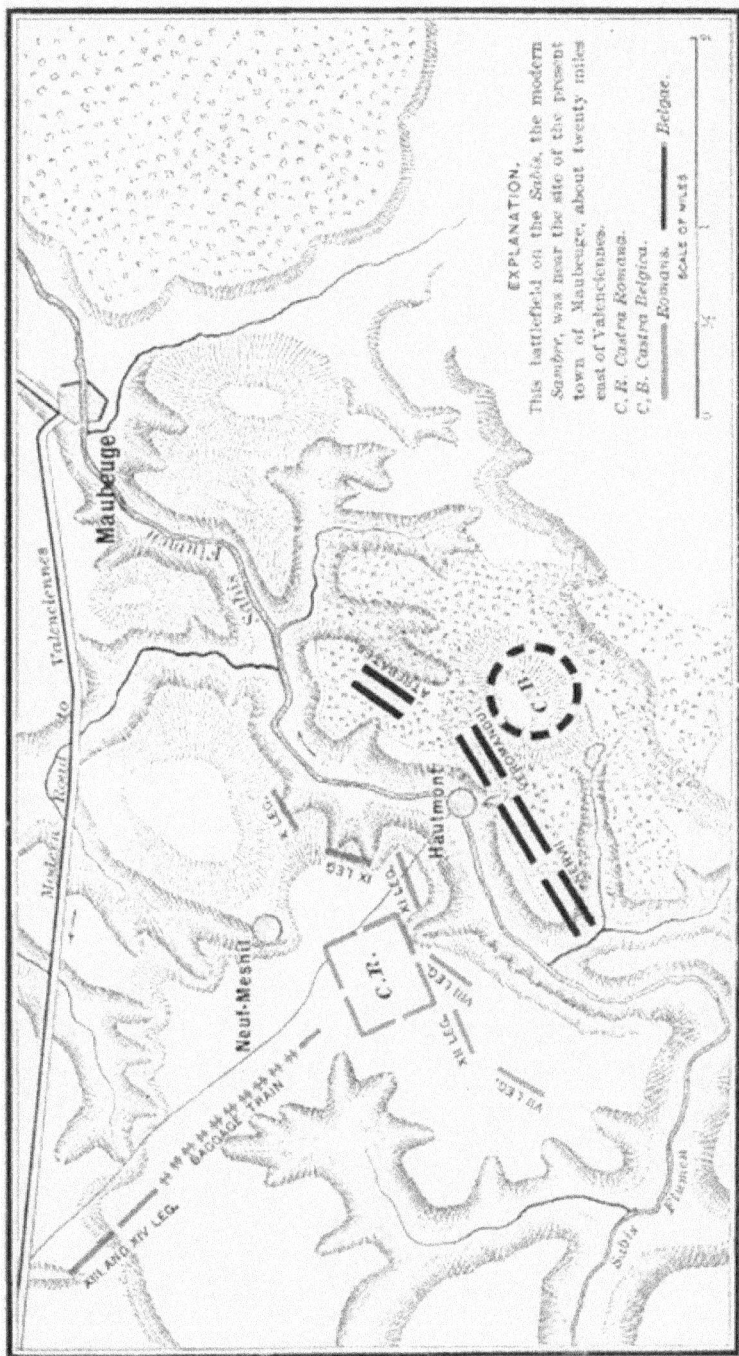

PLATE 10. BATTLE OF THE SABIS. 2 18—27

EXPLANATION.

This battlefield on the *Sabis*, the modern Sambre, was near the side of the present town of Maubeuge, about twenty miles east of Valenciennes.

C. R. *Castra Romana.*
C. B. *Castra Belgica.*

———— Romans.   ———— Belgae.

SCALE OF MILES

Maubeuge

Neuf-Mesnil

Haulmont

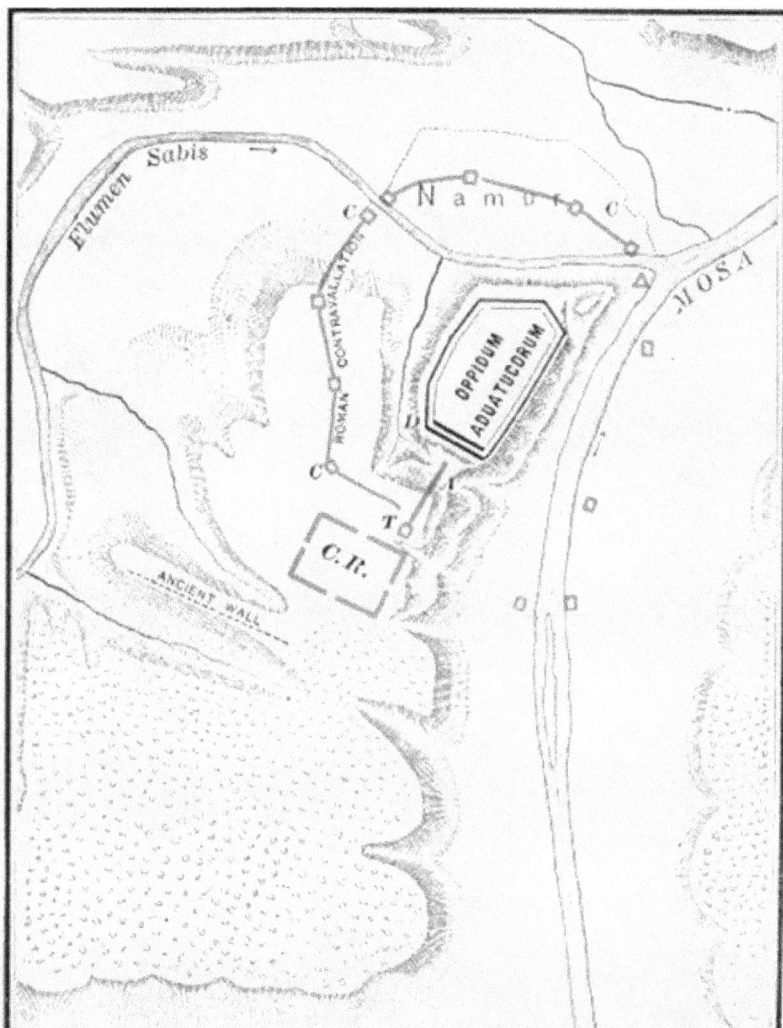

PLATE 11.SIEGE OF OPPIDTJM ADUATUCORUM. 2 29—33.

EXPLANATION.

This stronghold of the Aduatuci occupied the hill, on the right bank
of the *Sambre*, which now forms the citadel of *Namur*.

A. Roman *Agger.*

T. Turris ambulatoria.

C.C. Roman contravallation with numerous redoubts.

C, R. Castra Romana,

D. Double wall before the city.

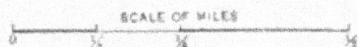

SCALE OF MILES

PLATE 12. EXPEDITION AGAINST THE VENETI. 3. 7—16

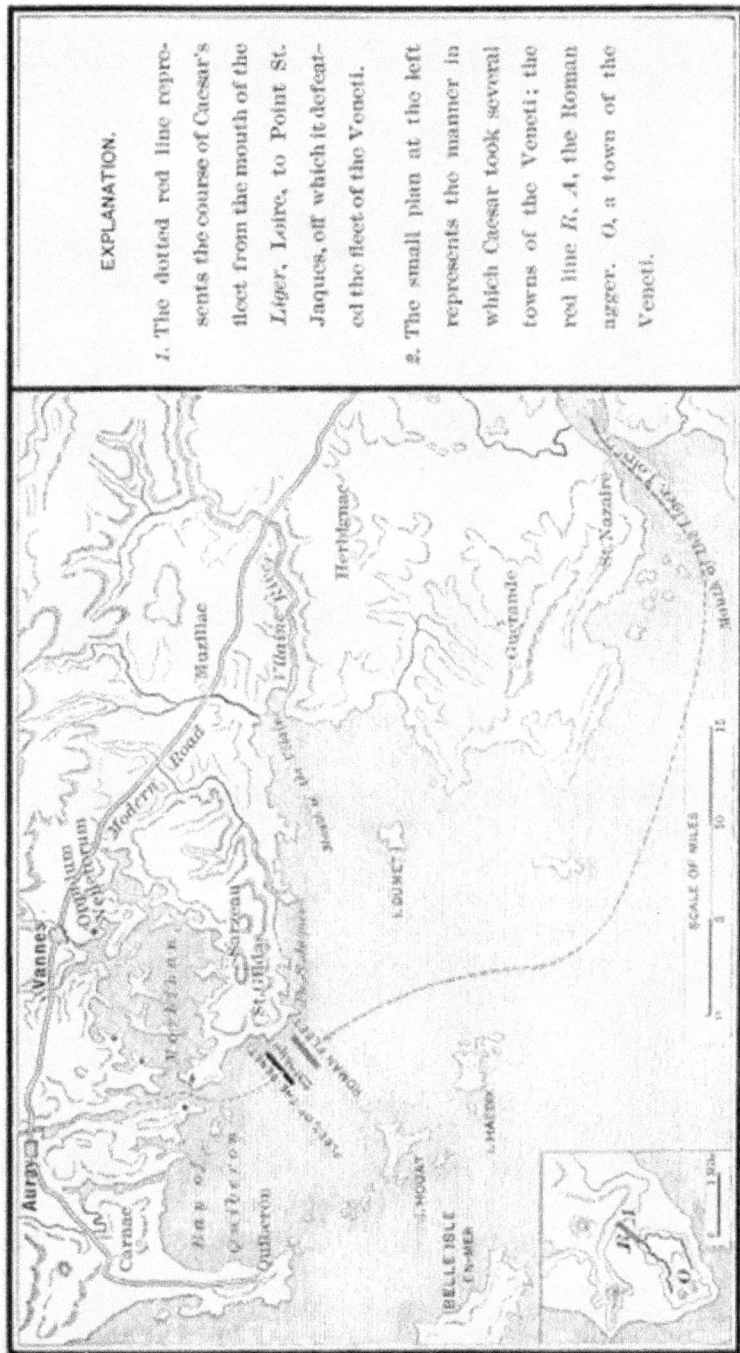

EXPLANATION.

1. The dotted red line represents the course of Caesar's fleet from the mouth of the *Liger*, Loire, to Point St. Jaques, off which it defeated the fleet of the Veneti.

2. The small plan at the left represents the manner in which Caesar took several towns of the Veneti; the red line *R, A,* the Roman agger. *O,* a town of the Veneti.

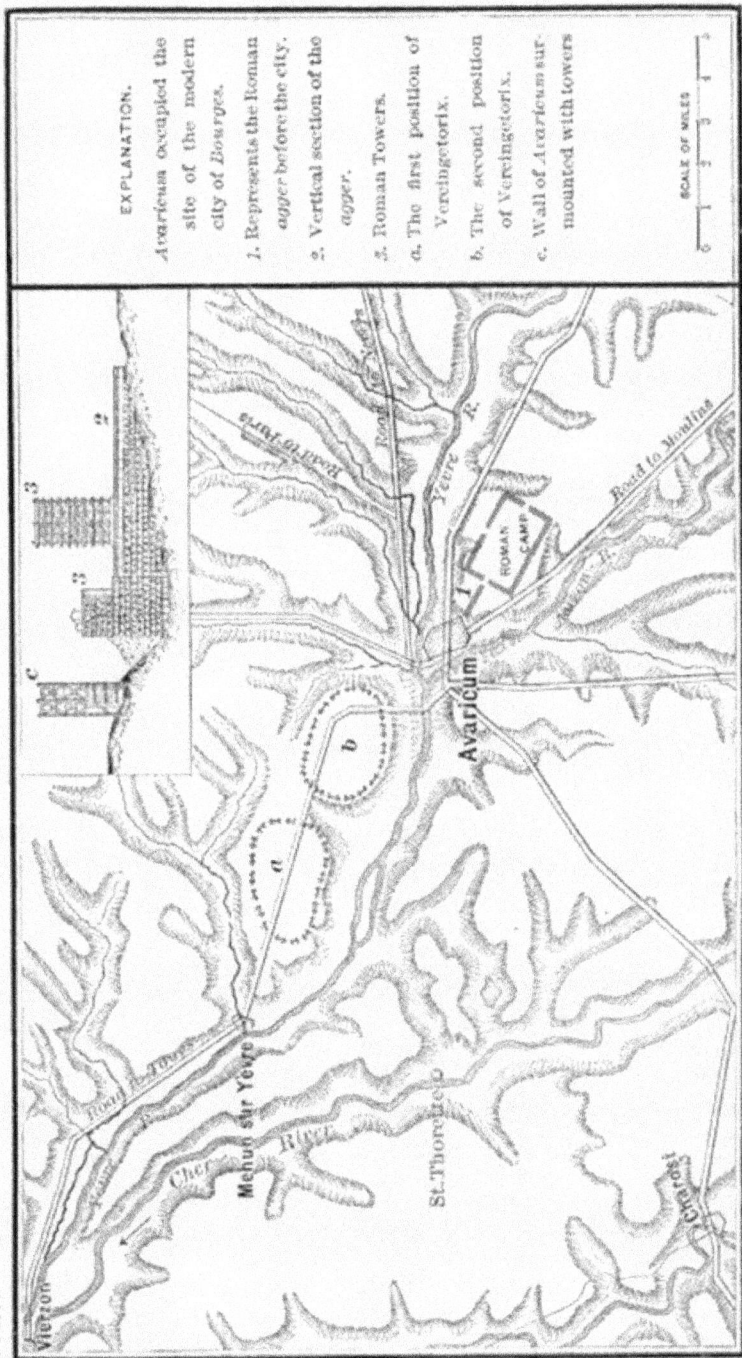

PLATE 13. SIEGE OF AVARICUM. 7. 16—30

EXPLANATION.

Avaricum occupied the
site of the modern
city of Bourges.

1. Represent the Roman
agger before the city.

2. Vertical section of the
agger.

3. Roman Towers.

a. The first position of
Vercingetorix.

b. The second position
of Vercingetorix.

c. Wall of Avaricum sur-
mounted with towers

SCALE OF MILES

Vierzon

Road to Tours

Cher
River

Mehun sur Yevre

St. Thorelieu

Avaricum

Yevre R.

ROMAN
CAMP

Auron R.

Road to Moulins

Charost

PLATE 14. SIEGE OF GERGOVIA. 7.36—52

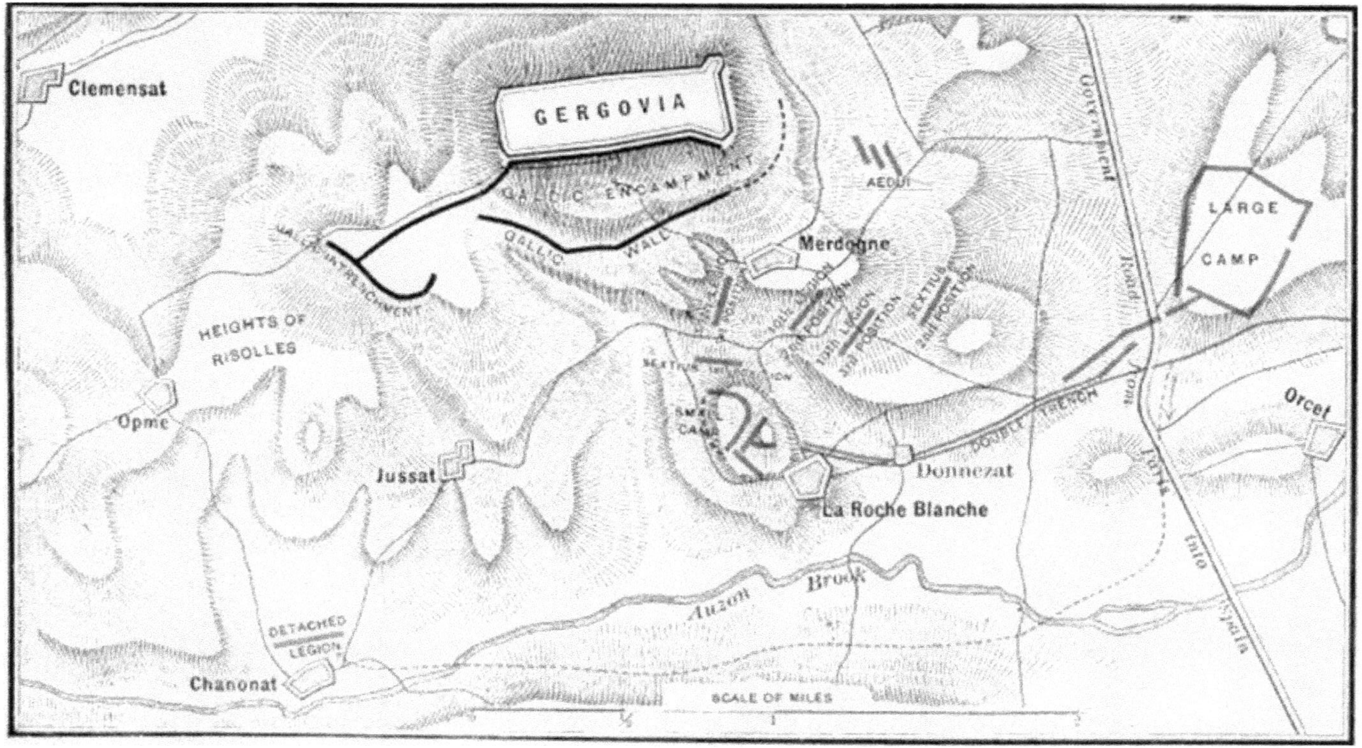

PLATE 14. EXPEDITION AGAINST LUTETIA. 7. 57—62.

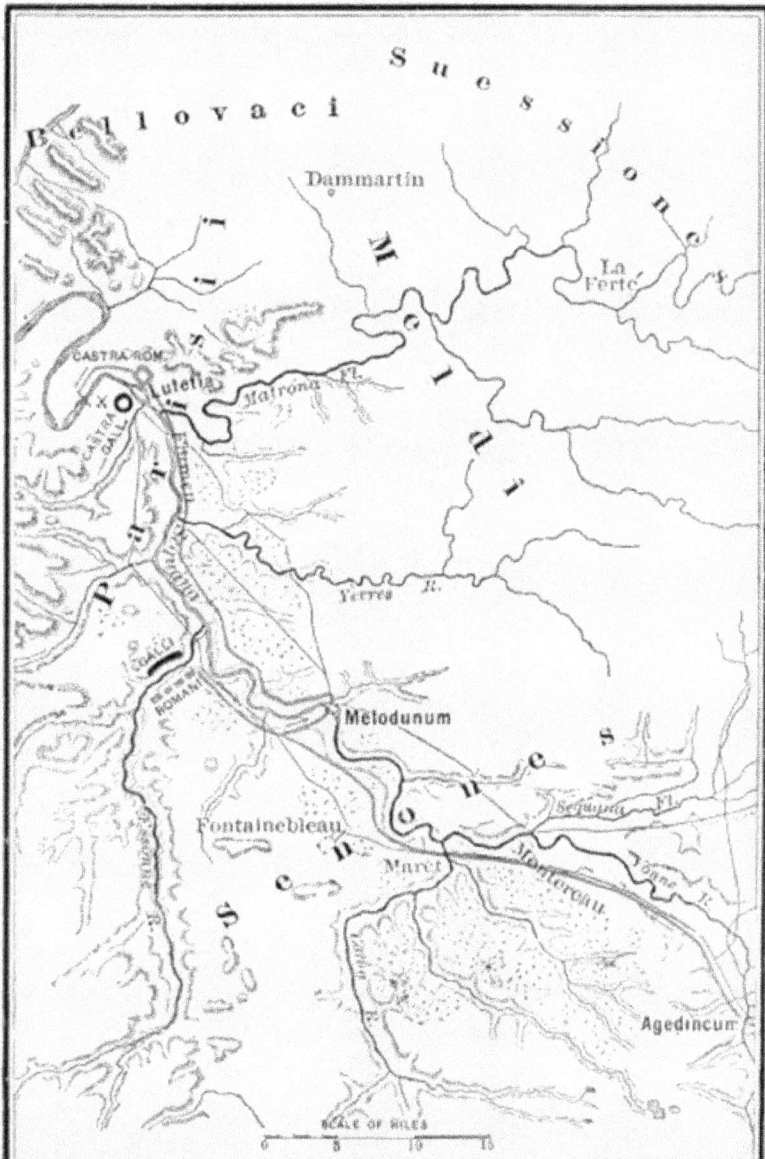

EXPLANATION.

Lutetia, *Paris*; Melodunum, *Melun*; Agedincum, *Sens*;
Sequana, *The Seine*; Matrona, *The Marne*; Castra Rom.,
Castra Romana; Castra Gall., *Castra Gallica*.

PLATE 16. VICTORY OVER VERCINGETORIX. 7. 66—67.

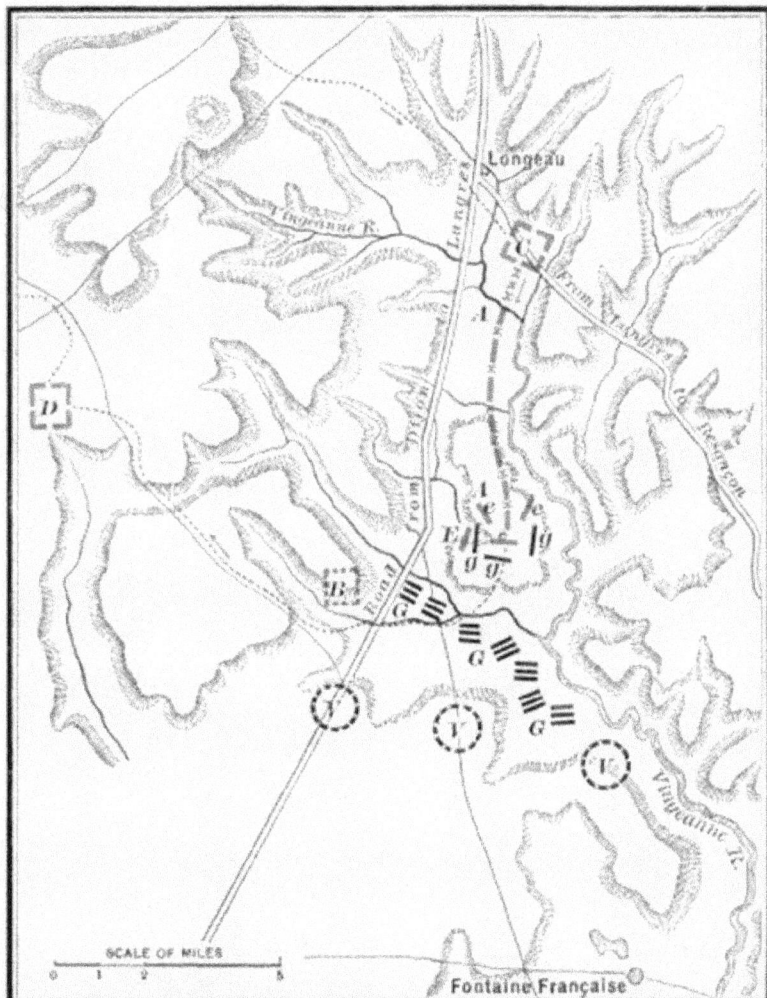

EXPLANATION.

A, A. Roman column on the march.
B. Baggage of the Romans.
C. Roman camp the night before the battle.
D. Roman camp the night after the battle.
c. Caesar's cavalry in three divisions.
E. German cavalry in Caesar's service.
g. The enemy's cavalry.
G. The enemy's infantry in line of battle.
V. The three camps of Vercingetorix.

PLATE 17. INVESTMENT OF ALESIA. 7. 68—90

EXPLANATION.

A, B, C. Infantry Camps on the Heights.
D. Camp of the two legions attacked by the Army of Relief.
G, H, I, K. Cavalry Camps near the water.
○ Redoubts.
J, J, J. Trench, 20 feet wide.
P, S. Gallic intrenchment.
✻ Caesar's position in the last battle.
Roman camps and works.

SCALE OF MILES

Rue du Veau
Rue du Pissot
Rue du Chateau
Bussy-le-Grand
Seigny
Ménétreux
Les Laumes
Venarey
Pouillenay
HEIGHTS OF BUSSY
HEIGHTS OF PENNEVELLE
HEIGHTS OF FLAVIGNY
ALESIA
Alise St. Reine
Flavigny
Dacey
Daccy
VALLEY LAUMES
CONTRAVALLATION
CIRCUMVALLATION
GALLIC ARMY OF RELIEF Mussy du Fosse
ROUTE OF THE GALLIC ARMY
Brenne R.
Oserain Brook
Rabutin Brook
Roman Road
Paris
Gresigny

LEONAUR

ALSO FROM LEONAUR

AVAILABLE IN SOFTCOVER OR HARDCOVER WITH DUST JACKET

THE RELUCTANT REBEL *by William G. Stevenson*—A young Kentuckian's experiences in the Confederate Infantry & Cavalry during the American Civil War..

BOOTS AND SADDLES *by Elizabeth B. Custer*—The experiences of General Custer's Wife on the Western Plains.

FANNIE BEERS' CIVIL WAR *by Fannie A. Beers*—A Confederate Lady's Experiences of Nursing During the Campaigns & Battles of the American Civil War.

LADY SALE'S AFGHANISTAN *by Florentia Sale*—An Indomitable Victorian Lady's Account of the Retreat from Kabul During the First Afghan War.

THE TWO WARS OF MRS DUBERLY *by Frances Isabella Duberly*—An Intrepid Victorian Lady's Experience of the Crimea and Indian Mutiny.

THE REBELLIOUS DUCHESS *by Paul F. S. Dermoncourt*—The Adventures of the Duchess of Berri and Her Attempt to Overthrow French Monarchy.

LADIES OF WATERLOO *by Charlotte A. Eaton, Magdalene de Lancey & Juana Smith*—The Experiences of Three Women During the Campaign of 1815: Waterloo Days by Charlotte A. Eaton, A Week at Waterloo by Magdalene de Lancey & Juana's Story by Juana Smith.

TWO YEARS BEFORE THE MAST *by Richard Henry Dana. Jr.*—The account of one young man's experiences serving on board a sailing brig—the Penelope—bound for California, between the years 1834-36.

A SAILOR OF KING GEORGE *by Frederick Hoffman*—From Midshipman to Captain—Recollections of War at Sea in the Napoleonic Age 1793-1815.

LORDS OF THE SEA *by A. T. Mahan*—Great Captains of the Royal Navy During the Age of Sail.

COGGESHALL'S VOYAGES: VOLUME 1 *by George Coggeshall*—The Recollections of an American Schooner Captain.

COGGESHALL'S VOYAGES: VOLUME 2 *by George Coggeshall*—The Recollections of an American Schooner Captain.

TWILIGHT OF EMPIRE *by Sir Thomas Ussher & Sir George Cockburn*—Two accounts of Napoleon's Journeys in Exile to Elba and St. Helena: Narrative of Events by Sir Thomas Ussher & Napoleon's Last Voyage: Extract of a diary by Sir George Cockburn.

LEONAUR

ALSO FROM LEONAUR
AVAILABLE IN SOFTCOVER OR HARDCOVER WITH DUST JACKET

ESCAPE FROM THE FRENCH by Edward Boys—A Young Royal Navy Midshipman's Adventures During the Napoleonic War.

THE VOYAGE OF H.M.S. PANDORA by Edward Edwards R. N. & George Hamilton, edited by Basil Thomson—In Pursuit of the Mutineers of the Bounty in the South Seas—1790-1791.

MEDUSA by J. B. Henry Savigny and Alexander Correard and Charlotte-Adélaïde Dard —Narrative of a Voyage to Senegal in 1816 & The Sufferings of the Picard Family After the Shipwreck of the Medusa.

THE SEA WAR OF 1812 VOLUME 1 by A. T. Mahan—A History of the Maritime Conflict.

THE SEA WAR OF 1812 VOLUME 2 by A. T. Mahan—A History of the Maritime Conflict.

WETHERELL OF H. M. S. HUSSAR by John Wetherell—The Recollections of an Ordinary Seaman of the Royal Navy During the Napoleonic Wars.

THE NAVAL BRIGADE IN NATAL by C. R. N. Burne—With the Guns of H. M. S. Terrible & H. M. S. Tartar during the Boer War 1899-1900.

THE VOYAGE OF H. M. S. BOUNTY by William Bligh—The True Story of an 18th Century Voyage of Exploration and Mutiny.

SHIPWRECK! by William Gilly—The Royal Navy's Disasters at Sea 1793-1849.

KING'S CUTTERS AND SMUGGLERS: 1700-1855 by E. Keble Chatterton—A unique period of maritime history-from the beginning of the eighteenth to the middle of the nineteenth century when British seamen risked all to smuggle valuable goods from wool to tea and spirits from and to the Continent.

CONFEDERATE BLOCKADE RUNNER by John Wilkinson—The Personal Recollections of an Officer of the Confederate Navy.

NAVAL BATTLES OF THE NAPOLEONIC WARS by W. H. Fitchett—Cape St. Vincent, the Nile, Cadiz, Copenhagen, Trafalgar & Others.

PRISONERS OF THE RED DESERT by R. S. Gwatkin-Williams—The Adventures of the Crew of the Tara During the First World War.

U-BOAT WAR 1914-1918 by James B. Connolly/Karl von Schenk—Two Contrasting Accounts from Both Sides of the Conflict at Sea D uring the Great War.

www.ingramcontent.com/pod-product-compliance
Lightning Source LLC
Chambersburg PA
CBHW032021090426
42741CB00006B/687